YOU CAN TEACH YOURSELF
HARMONICA

By George Heaps-Nelson
& Barbara McClintock Koehler

Dedication
This book is respectfully dedicated to George Keller, who always had time for me.

Acknowledgments
We've enjoyed every moment of preparing this manuscript — but it would never have happened without the patience and continual support of our esteemed spouses, Marilyn Heaps-Nelson and Bill Koehler. Our thanks to Porter Horne, who kept the proper beats in the measures, and to Geri Horne for her folky graphics. Also thanks to our photographers, Alice Owens and Bob McClintock. Thanks to all our friends at the Library of Congress, especially Joe Hickerson and the folks in the Archive of Folk Music. Special thanks to Susie Gilley for keeping all our bad little boys, Jimmy, Tommy, Chris, Keith, and Kenny, out of our hair! Thanks to our patient typist and re-typist, Diana Simon. Last but certainly not least, our thanks to Eric Muller for his expertise and to Bill Bay of Mel Bay Publications for his patience and help.

AUTHORS: Barbara McClintock Koehler and George Heaps-Nelson

Photo by Bob McClintock

PREFACE

One day in the marble playing season of 1956, April probably, possibly May, my grandfather gave me a dollar. After finding the necessary tax pennies in my "junk drawer" I set out with my older brother Dave to get a harmonica. There was no music store in my hometown so we went downtown to the drugstore where I bought the only Hohner one dollar could buy, a Vest Pocket Harp in C. I learned to play *Oh Susanna*, *The Old Grey Mare*, and *My Old Kentucky Home* in the next few weeks and was perfectly happy playing those three songs for the next several years. Later when I began to take a stronger interest in the music of my area, I would pick up a tune from one player, a tongue technique from another, and a flourish from a third. I continue to believe that this type of learning experience is very important for anyone who wants to play folk music. I also believe however that a more systematic and rapid approach is possible and I sincerely hope that this book will help to provide it. Enjoy yourself. Play what you like, skip what you don't, and take everyone, including me, with a grain of salt. Good luck, and may your stuck reeds be few and far between.

George Heaps-Nelson

When my husband and I opened our retail music store in Gainesville, Florida near the University, we little realized how much innate talent was to be found among the students.

Working with George in doing this book has really been a happy experience for me. Behind the serious Ph.D. rests a very fine musician and a beautiful person.

I actually (in my role as lady-editor-rewrite-typist-coordinator) now really am just beginning to appreciate the sensitivity of the harp. Hopefully this book will bring musical rewards to all of you.

Barbara McClintock Koehler

A cassette tape with most of the songs from this book is available. The publisher strongly recommends the use of this cassette along with the text to insure accuracy of interpretation and ease in learning.

If the cassette was not included as part of a book/cassette package; it is available from:

Sunny Mountain Records
P.O. Box 14592
Gainesville, FL 32604
or
Mel Bay Publications, Inc.
P.O. Box 66
Pacific, MO 63069-0066

Photo Courtesy M. Hohner Co.

4

TABLE OF CONTENTS

Sharecropper's Daughter, 1938
Photo by R. Lee, Library of Congress Collection

CHAPTER I INTRODUCTION

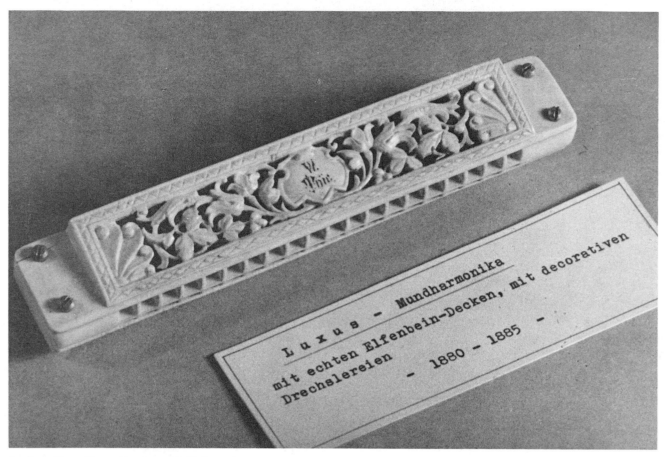

Antique Harp Photo Courtesy M. Hohner Co.

This book is written to help the person who wants to play American folk music or the blues on the harmonica.

Several different styles are analyzed and representative tunes are given each of them. Within the various sections the songs are roughly graded as to difficulty. An extra section examines some specialized techniques and introduces some harmonicas other than the standard ten-hole-twenty-reed diatonic harp for which most of the songs in this book are written.

"Why learn folk music or blues from a book?" you ask. That's a good question. We've never known or heard of a really good folk musician who didn't do a good bit of his learning from interaction with other musicians. On the other hand, an instruction book like this can be useful for several reasons. First, it can get a beginner started while he is looking for musicians to get together with. This is important because most folk musicians, especially harmonica players, are amateurs who do honest work for a living and who don't go around with a sign that says "TRADITIONAL FOLK MUSICIAN'-Disciples Wanted."

Secondly, a book can get you started to the point where, at most, you may have something to contribute to the musical circle and at least you'll have some basis for asking reasonable, intelligent questions. The experienced musician would much rather hear "How'd you do that flutter at the beginning of *Casey Jones*?" than "Will you teach me to play the harmonica?"

Thirdly, you may want to expand your playing to include styles not common to your area. When I was learning to play harmonica in Northwest Iowa there were good men to learn from but nobody played the blues there. I never did figure out the basics of blues techniques until I left that region and went to California. A good written explanation of cross harp would have been quite welcome.

Lastly, the musicians you find to play with probably learned by trial and error and are not likely to be extremely analytical and articulate about their playing. I know this is true because in writing this book I have had to analyze and define many things that I had previously taken for granted.

If any of these four reasons apply to you, this book may well be a big help to you. The key word here is "help". Folk and Blues Harmonica is an aid, not a method. Have fun learning and playing!

Herb Carlisle, Gainesville, Florida
Photo by Alice Owens

Granny Wiggins, Age 94
Photo by Bill Shields—The Gainesville Sun

Colonel Charlie Wellborn,
Gainesville, Florida
Photo by Bob McClintock

8

FINDING FOLKS TO LEARN FROM

Where do I find these traditional musicians to learn from, you ask? Another good question. If you want to play blues there shouldn't be too much of a problem. There are many fine records of blues harp players (see the Discography) and in addition there are many good musicians around playing blues harp. Furthermore, blues players tend to be highly noticeable people; they play in bars, jook joints, clubs, concerts etc. These audience-performer relationships generate publicity and your search is thereby made easier.

Street Scene
Library of Congress Collection

Harmonica players in the Anglo-American tradition may be harder to find. Though sometimes present in old timey string bands and commercial country music (again see the Discography) the traditional white harmonica player is very often a living room musician playing mostly for his own amazement as one of my friends likes to say. Television, the generation gap, and our preoccupation with things up-to-date has made these musicians hard to find.

The Harmonica Lesson
Photo by Bob McClintock

Senior Citizens Fun and Fellowship Harmonica Band
Photo by Vernon Rathell

Some suggestions about where to look? Go to the old time fiddle conventions and contests, community talent nights and musically oriented neighborhood taverns. Ask music store owners about who buys harmonicas. Keep your eyes open. While looking remember that in addition to the harmonica's popularity as a folk instrument it enjoyed a great vogue as a music education tool in the years between 1920 and 1950. The veterans of the school harmonica band years must be out there somewhere and they may have a lot to show you.

"A harmonica is easy to carry. Take it out of your hip pocket, knock it against your palm to shake out the dirt and pocket fuzz and bits of tobacco. Now it's ready. You can do anything with a harmonica: thin reedy single tones, or chords, or melody with rhythm chords. You can mold the music with curved hands, making it wail and cry like bagpipes, making it full and round like an organ, making it as sharp and bitter as the reed pipes of the hills. And you can play and put it back in your pocket. And it is always with you, always in your pocket. And as you play, you learn new tricks, new ways to mold the tone with your hands, to pinch the tone with your lips, and no one teaches you. You feel around — sometimes alone in the shade at noon, sometimes in the tent door after supper when the women are washing up. Your foot taps gently on the ground. Your eyebrows rise and fall in rhythm. And if you lose or break it, why it's no great loss. You can buy another for a quarter."

John Steinbeck, *Grapes of Wrath*
published by Viking Press

Pennsylvania Homesteader, 1937
Photo by B. Shahn, Library of Congress Collection

Harmonicas don't cost a quarter anymore but they're still readily available and relatively inexpensive. Now, assuming that you, the authors and John Steinbeck are all in agreement that the harmonica is a nice sort of thing, we can go on to talk about how this book should be used.

The songs and instruction in this book are written for a 10 hole 20 reed diatonic harmonica in the key of C. Such an instrument is composed of a small box with two metal plates inside and a comb of wood, plastic, or metal that separates them. Each of these plates has 10 reeds attached to it. The reeds on the bottom plate are activated when you draw ↓ air through the instrument, the ones on the top, when you blow ↑. Thus each hole can sound two notes, one blow and one draw, giving us 20 notes to work with.

All of the songs are given in two notation systems, standard musical notation and a numbers and arrows system developed by Thomas Hart Benton (used with permission of the M. Hohner Co.) in which the numbers signify the holes in the harmonica (1-10) left to right (bass on the left), and the arrows denote both direction of air flow (blow ↑ or draw ↓) and the proper amount of time to hold the note.*

The advantages of each system are perhaps obvious. Learning standard notation will enable you to pick up melody lines from books, greatly expanding your ability to learn new songs. The arrows and holes system is perhaps simpler. In addition it frees you from anything resembling formal music instruction. This can be quite important if you have bad memories of piano teachers who pasted little bluebirds on your kiddie piano books to show that you were a dutiful obedient child — likely to grow up to be a credit to his parents — ever mindful of the many hours they labored and sacrifices they endured to provide their cherished offspring with music lessons etc. ad nausem.

For the reasons already mentioned I prefer standard notation but I certainly wouldn't twist your arm about it. It does require memorizing the staff and understanding the time value of notes. For a detailed explanation of this, see Appendix I.

A line without a point indicates that the note in question should sound as an unbroken continuation of the previous note.

Harmonicas 25¢
Photo Courtesy M. Hohner Co.

Here's a diagram of the ten hole C harmonica*
done in holes and arrows, musical notation and
do-re-mi, etc. thrown in if you like to think that
way. All these notes are written an octave lower
than they really sound to avoid too many notes
above the staff.

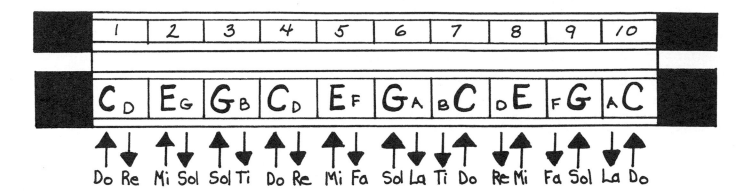

*A C harmonica is only necessary if you are going
to read music or learn with the record. With the
numbers and arrows systems any key will do fine.

Note that in the bottom octave F and A are not
there and in the top one B is missing. This limits
us in some ways but also makes some nice things
possible as we'll see later on. The middle octave is
a complete C to C scale.

October, 1940
Photo by Post-Wolcott, Library of Congress Collection

Photo by Alice Owens

Photo Courtesy M. Hohner Co.

WHAT KIND OF HARMONICA SHOULD YOU BUY?

It is my opinion that the Golden Melody harmonica, made by M. Hohner Co. is the best one available today. Why? Its reeds are far superior to those on any other diatonic making for a much richer sound. It also has a hard plastic playing surface that doesn't absorb saliva and swell (a problem with those instruments that have wooden combs).

Golden Melody Harp
Photo Courtesy M. Hohner Co.

Arist-O-Kratt Harp
Photo Courtesy William Kratt Co.

Warbler Harp
Photo Courtesy William Kratt Co.

There are five other harmonicas that I feel make excellent choices. The best buys among them are the Arist-O-Kratt and the Warbler, both made by the American firm William Kratt and Co. They have plastic combs, good response and are the least expensive good harmonicas on the market.

The other three are other Hohner Products. The Marine Band is probably the best selling harmonica in the U.S. today and has long been the standard by which harmonicas are judged. The Hohner Blues Harp is a super responsive edition of the Marine Band. Designed for playing the blues, it is also nice for playing fiddle tunes, especially in the higher keys. Hohner's Orchestra I is also a good harp; it has a metal comb, again avoiding the problems of soaked swollen wood.

Both companies make less expensive harmonicas that are acceptable for beginners but which are usually lacking in tone and response. There may be other suitable harps around. If you find them, more power to you.

Marine Band Harp
Photo Courtesy M. Hohner Co.

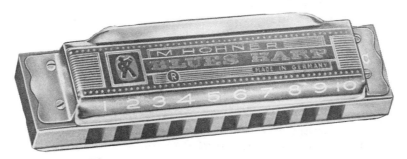

Blues Harp
Photo Courtesy M. Hohner Co.

15

PROLONGING THE LIFE OF YOUR HARMONICA

Harmonicas don't last forever. Eventually they begin to lose both tone and pitch. Here are a few ways to prolong harmonica life.

1. **Play with a clean mouth.**

2. **Don't play extremely forcefully or loud when the harmonica is new. You can wreck the reeds that way.**

3. **Hang on to the box. Maybe you won't get all that tobacco and pocket fuzz in it.**

4. **Blues players usually soak their harmonica in water. This gives a nice sound, shortens the life of the harp and can make the instrument go slightly sharp.**

5. **Stuck reeds can be freed by taking the harmonica apart and wiggling things about with a one sided razor blade. (As Michael Cooney has pointed out, the Kratt harmonicas score here for they are easier to take apart and put back together than the Hohner harmonicas.)**

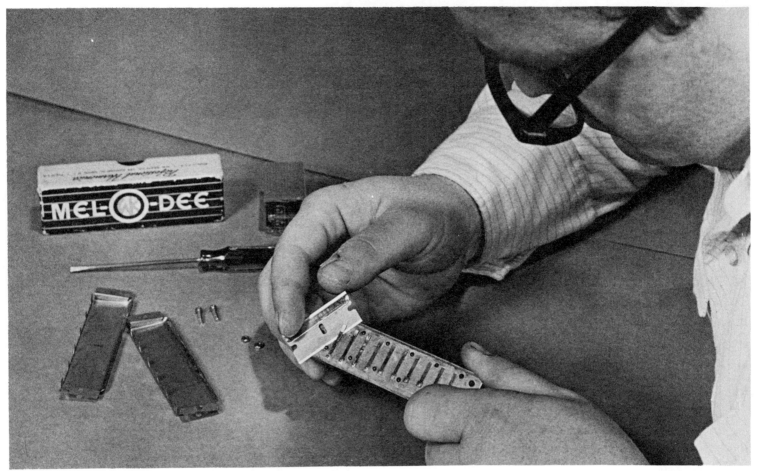

Taken Apart Harp
Photo by Alice Owens

Extra tip:

Heavy smoking can cut down on your wind, making it harder to play good harmonica. Drinking and evil companions probably aren't too good for you either though a certain dissoluteness can add a touch of authenticity to hard luck songs and sad blues.

Second extra tip:

If your town doesn't have a music store (mine didn't) there may be harmonicas available at the drug store or in a tavern.

Third extra tip:

No one's quality control is what is should be. Don't accept defective harps. If the friendly storekeeper gets nasty send the harp back to the manufacturer.

Now get in there and make music!

CHAPTER II
GETTIN' STARTED

Scarecrow
Photo by Dave Whitsen

I know of three good ways of holding the harmonica, they are illustrated here with photos.   Take your choice.

Outside Position "A"
Photo by Alice Owens

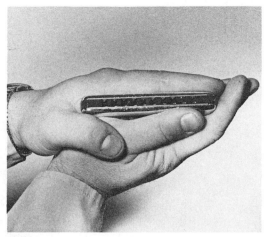

Inside Position "A"
Photo by Alice Owens

Outside Position "B"
Photo by Alice Owens

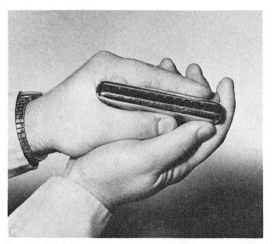

Inside Position "B"
Photo by Alice Owens

Outside Position "C"
Photo by Alice Owens

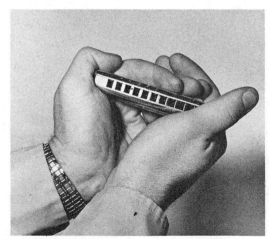

Inside Position "C"
Photo by Alice Owens

There are two ways of getting a single note out of the harmonica. Method 1 is to purse the lips until only one note sounds. A fleshy lower lip can help here. If you have one, you can turn the harmonica face slightly down into the lip.

Method 2 is called tongue blocking. It makes chording possible later and is somewhat more flexible than the pursed lips method. To play a single tone in this manner put your mouth around three holes and block off the two to the left with your tongue. (Some folks say that you should cover four holes with your lips and block off the lower three. It makes no difference, don't worry about it.) If you now blow or draw, a single note should sound. Now follow the numbers and arrows and play the song.

SKIP TO MY LOU

This is an old play party tune that can sound good on the harmonica. If you are young and hip and think it's a rinky dink sissy song, listen to Sonny Terry play it on Folkways FA2201.

SKIP TO MY LOU I

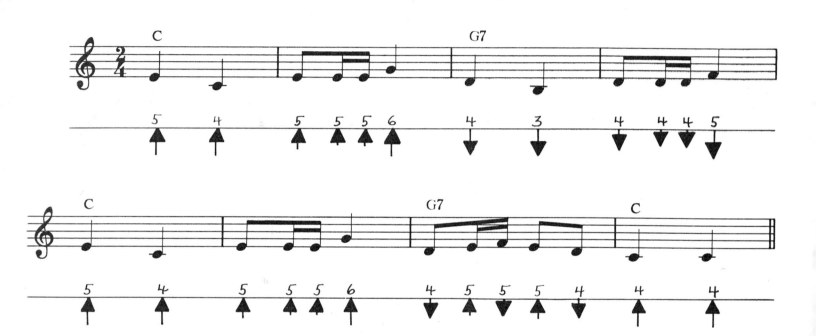

If the second line with all its draw notes bothers you, you can condition yourself by seeing how many short draw notes you can play in a row without exhaling. If the tongue blocking is really hard for you try the other way for awhile, periodically returning to tongue blocking until you get it down. Believe me it's very useful to know. I once knew a guy who blocked off the notes to the right rather than those to the left. The only difference is that later on you'll get high chords rather than lower ones to go with the melody.

At any rate concentrate on single notes for awhile and play the first three songs in the next chapter.

Farm Auction, 1939
Photo by J. Vachon, Library of Congress Collection

CHAPTER III
BALLADS AND FOLK TUNES

The first three songs presented in this section are well known folk songs, all ideally suited to the quiet tone "lonesome" variety of harmonica playing. *Oh Shenandoah* should be played quite freely, rather than with strong rhythmic emphasis. If guitar accompaniment is used, it should be simple and equally free. *Streets of Laredo* has a more definite 3/4 or waltz type rhythm, while *Colorado Trail* is even, medium 4/4. Both of these last tunes go nicely with a steady bass-chord or bass-arpeggio accompaniment. Try for a clear sweet single tone on these songs, whether you're playing the tongue blocking or pursed lips method.

When you've got them down pretty well, or before that point if you like, add some vibrato, particularly on the half and whole notes. To obtain vibrato first check diagram to make sure you are holding the harmonica in one of the three indicated positions. In any of these positions you are playing the harmonica inside a chamber formed by your face and hands. Next, play a long single tone rapidly opening and closing that chamber with the right hand. The tone and pitch change very quickly, giving a quavering sound that can be nice on the slow pieces.

How much vibrato? Well, that's a matter of taste but I'd say don't overdo it.

Some other good tunes, which you can find out about by yourself are: *Red River Valley, Bury Me Not On The Lone Prairie, The Storms Are On The Ocean* and *Cowboy Jack.* Look for them, it'll do you good.

OH SHENANDOAH

People who know more about folk songs than I do say this was originally a sea chantey; they're probably right.

O SHENANDOAH

STREETS OF LAREDO

This one is about a young cowboy getting moral on his death bed. I've given the tune twice, once in the middle octave and once in the higher range. Alternating the two octaves makes for variety.

Photo by Alice Owens

STREETS OF LAREDO I

"Adapted and Arranged By George Heaps - Nelson,"

STREETS OF LAREDO II

"Adapted and Arranged By George Heaps - Nelson,"

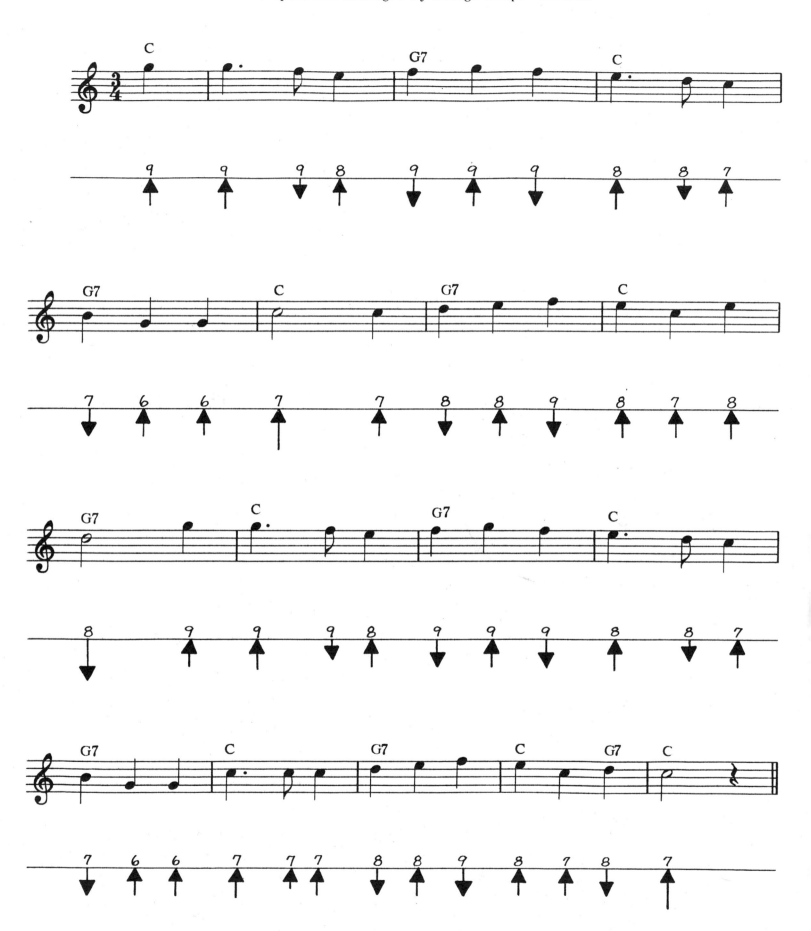

COLORADO TRAIL

Adapted and Arranged By George Heaps - Nelson,

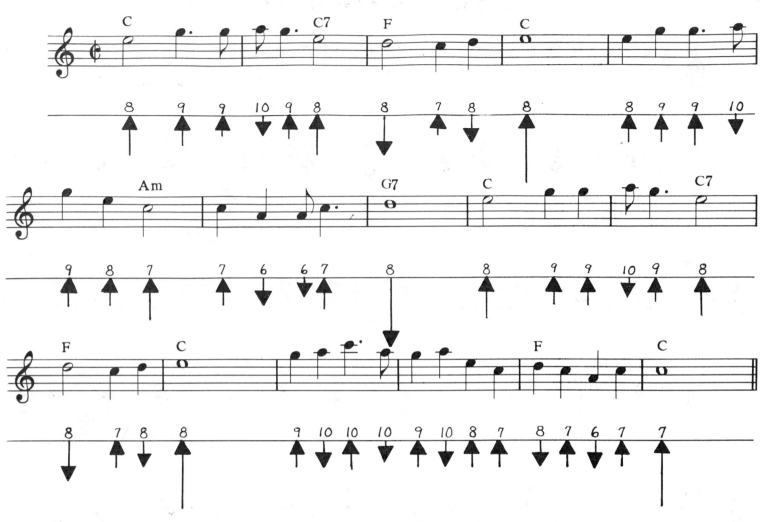

Perhaps that sixth measure should go like this instead:

Alternate 6th Measure

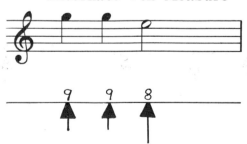

COLORADO TRAIL

Colorado Trail is unplayable in the usual middle range of the harmonica because it drops to the A that is left out of the bottom octave. In the higher octave, it is playable and can sound quite nice. If it seems too high for you, maybe you'd like to try it on a G or A harp. The Marine Band Soloist (discussed in the Etc. section) is another possibility.

The last line could be different too, like this:

Alternate ending

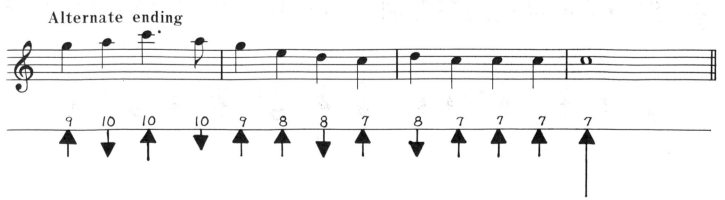

If you've been working on your tongue blocking you're ready to play chords with the melody now. Play a clear single note, periodically pulling the tongue back from the playing surface and quickly replacing it there. When the tongue is removed from the two holes it rests on, more notes sound, giving you a chord below the melody note. I find that chords sound best if they're clipped short and precise; otherwise things can get muddy sounding. If you're having trouble make sure the harp is well into your mouth. Also don't worry about how many notes your chords have. I have written the music assuming two — but if you have a bigger mouth or thinner lips than I do, there may be three.

Here's *Skip To My Lou* again, this time with chords added. In the numbers and arrows notation the momentary tongue movement that produces a chord will appear as an L (L as in Lift your tongue).

SKIP TO MY LOU II

Adapted and Arranged By George Heaps - Nelson

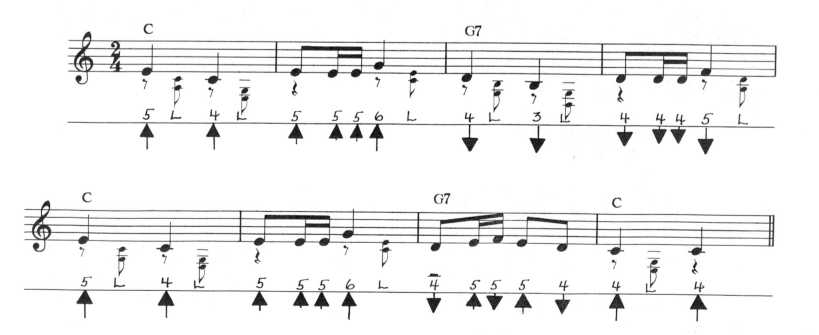

Rovin' Gambler, The Prisoners Lament, and *Rye Whiskey* are almost as well known as the four preceding songs. They have more rhythmic punch however, and make good tunes for a string band replete with guitar and banjo accompaniment.

Maybe you could trade solos with a fiddler. Remember, when you're playing with a singer, back off a little and don't do everything you know how to do.

I have indicated some spots where chords thrown in would be nice. If you like the idea, put them in. Don't let your renditions get overly regular or cluttered up with chords; the former is boring and the latter distracting.

Other tunes that go nicely with chords are: *Home Sweet Home, Worried Man Blues, The FFV,* and *Columbus Stockade Blues.* That last tune might be a little hard to find in a book, but easy to find at a gathering of Old Time musicians.

A cool drink from the pond
Photo by Dave Whitsen

No Hunting or Trespassing
Photo by Dave Whitsen

ROVIN' GAMBLER

Adapted and Arranged By George Heaps - Nelson

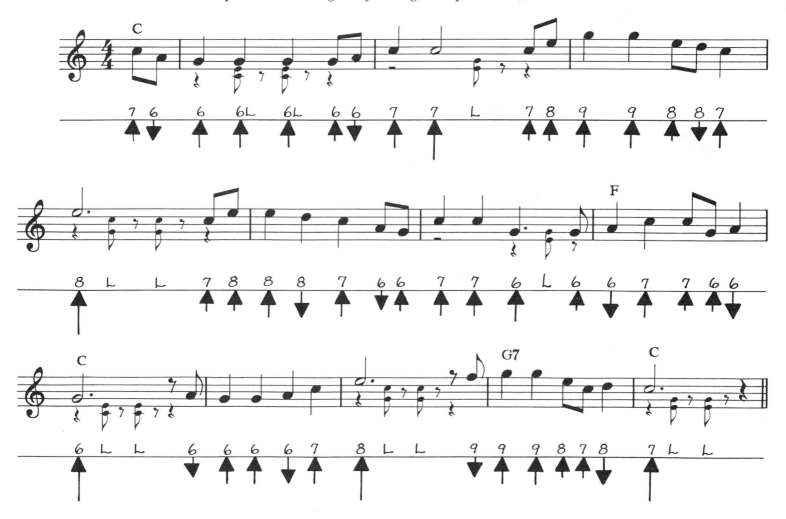

Photo by Marcus Johnson

THE PRISONER'S LAMENT

Adapted and Arranged By George Heaps - Nelson,

RYE WHISKY

"Adapted and Arranged By George Heaps - Nelson,"

Troubled Man, 1938
Photo by B. Shahn, Library of Congress Collection

As your playing becomes more natural, try for some of the tonal variety that Steinbeck was talking about. Alternate the pursed lips and the tongue blocking methods in the same song to see what a difference it can make. Pursed lips when combined with extra pressure can give you a shrill forceful sound while less breath or tongue blocking will result in mellower tones. (You'll notice this throughout on the companion record for this book.) Experiment. Your harp has a wide range of possibilities.

The next three tunes are a little harder. They are very good for when you feel like strutting your stuff a little or when you have to get the attention of audiences that are blase' and bored, or drunk and unruly. Any ordinary kind of string band accompaniment is fine, though I really like to hear a washboard and guitar backing up *Round The Bend*. All three songs have to do with railroads and railroading so you might want to use a few chugging sounds on the low end of the harmonica for introductions. I've never heard any two harmonica players do train sounds alike, so just experiment into the low end of your harp, with syllables like "chucka chucka" (good for blow) or "lucka lucka" (good for draw) or "hiddley hiddley" (good for either).

When you get the train sound going, draw hard on holes 3 and 4 for the whistle, then end up the train rhythm with some blow chords and start your song. Some good tunes which can work as "show pieces" are *Wildwood Flower, Fireball Mail, The Big Rock Candy Mountain*, and *Listen to the Mockingbird*.

THE WRECK OF THE OLD 97

The Wreck of the Old 97 is a good example of the disaster songs which were so popular among the country people in the early part of this century. There's nothing too tricky about it, just more chords than in the previous songs and somewhat catchier tune.

Photo by Alice Owens

34

THE WRECK OF THE OLD 97

Adapted and Arranged By George Heaps - Nelson,

THE WABASH CANNONBALL

The Wabash Cannonball is an old hobo song that's widely known among folk and country musicians. The words are sung in many different ways, but the tune is usually fairly similar from one bunch of pickers to another. Always be prepared to give a little when playing with a group. Arguments about the rightness of one version or another are quite unpleasant and usually unproductive.

Bag On Depot Step
Photo by Marcus Johnson

WABASH CANNONBALL

"Adapted and Arranged By George Heaps - Nelson,"

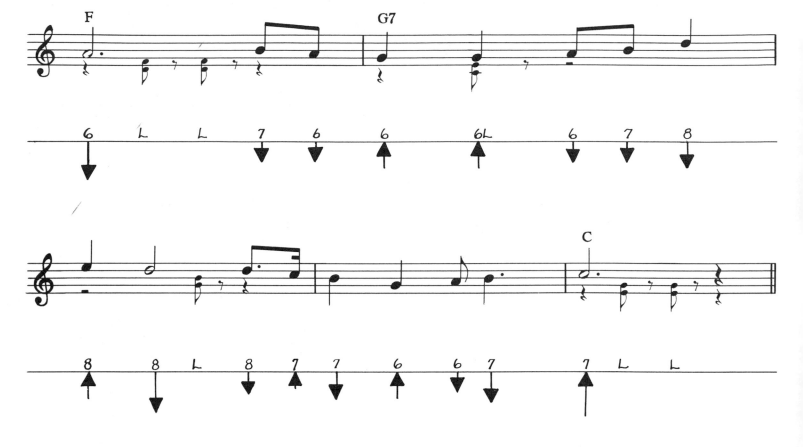

WABASH CANNONBALL

Adapted and Arranged By George Heaps - Nelson,

Alternate 1st phrase

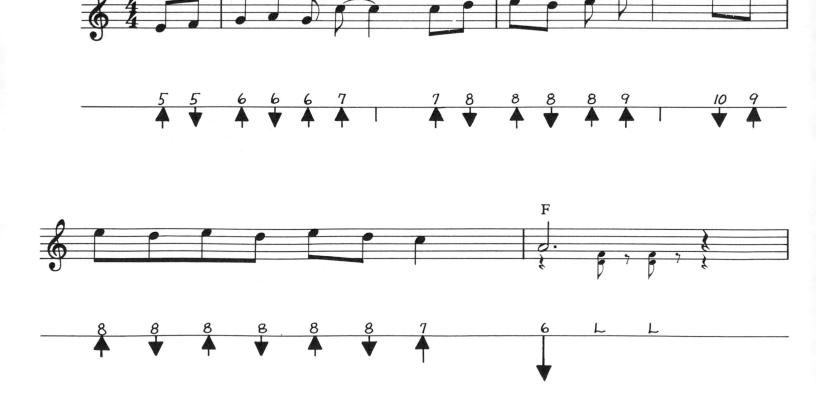

Photo by Alice Owens

Round the Bend is an old member of the folk song family that eventually produced *Casey Jones*.

The version presented here can be a real harmonica players showpiece. There are several special techniques that go well with this song. The first is a very rapid tongue flutter, called the double shuffle by one of my old friends back home. If you know a Spanish speaking person, get him to say the word for dog in Spanish. He will say "perro" with a rolled "r". That is exactly the movement you are looking for. Children very often use the same movement when asked to describe the purring of a cat. Work on it and put it in the song where you see the word "flutter" over the notes. It's a nice extra but not absolutely necessary. Don't jump out of a tall building if you don't get it right away.

Very simplistic full chords are another nice feature of this rendition. Notice that unlike the chords in previous songs, these are not connected by one long sustained note above them, they are separated and even somewhat choppy. This staccato sound is gained by explosive quick breathing (to get the idea say hah hah hah so forcefully that your whole torso seems to bounce), combined with emphatic tapping of the tongue on the appropriate hole.

When your chords remind you of a series of sharp hammer taps, you are getting there. I like the effect very much. If you like it, you'll probably find some other good places to use it (you could drop back and try it on *The Wabash Cannonball*).

Have a look at the song *Frankie and Johnny* in the last chapter. If you have a blues-harmonica-playing-friend, you might want to use the duet technique described there. In *Frankie and Johnny* the blues accompaniment is a counter melody. Here you could use a simpler series of chords, long held notes and train whistles.

Railroad Station - Bell, Florida
Photo by Alice Owens

ROUND THE BEND

Arr. by GEORGE HEAPS-NECSON

Fiddler - Upstate New York
Photo by Jim Lloyd

CHAPTER IV
FIDDLE TUNES

The songs presented in this chapter are traditional British-American dance tunes — commonly called fiddle tunes. They range in difficulty from *Uncle Joe*, which is considerably easier to play than some of the songs in the first chapter, to *The Wild Horse at Stoney Point*, which is a bit of a tongue twister. Most of these tunes have two parts which are marked A and B. Quite often each part is played twice, making an AABB pattern.

If you enjoy these tunes and have been using the holes and arrows system, this might be a good time to reconsider your decision not to learn to read music. There are quite a number of books which contain good fiddle tunes written out in musical notation; that might be a handy way to pick up more songs. Go to your local music store or write to us for recommendations on what books to pick up. If you do start reading music don't let it hold you down any. Just use it to get a notion of what the tune is like and then take off on your own.

Picking up a few more harps might be appropriate now, especially if you play with a string band. G,A,C,D and E will take care of most situations, though I usually have an F, a Bb, and a B also around somewhere. If you want an F harp I strongly recommend the Hohner Blues Harp with its easy action. Other F harps tend to be stiff.

Homesteader - South Dakota, 1937
Photo by A. Rothstein, Library of Congress Collection

MISS McCLOUD'S REEL

Miss McCloud's Reel, known in other versions as *Uncle Joe*, *Mrs. MacLeod's Reel*, *Ms. McCloud's Reel*, and *Hop High Ladies — The Cake's All Dough*, is a fairly easy song to play — I learned it from Donald McDowell of Layfayette, Indiana. It incorporates one musical form we haven't talked about so far, the triplet. A triplet divides the beat in three rather than one, two or four as is usual. The triplet is marked ⌒3⌒ in standard musical notation. Perhaps I can best explain how it sounds by a pattern of syllables. The first seven notes should go something like da da diddley da da, counted out it would be two-and-one-and-a-two-and.

44

MISS McCLOUD'S REEL

"Adapted and Arranged By George Heaps - Nelson,"

MISS McCLOUDS REEL

Alternate version for last three measures:

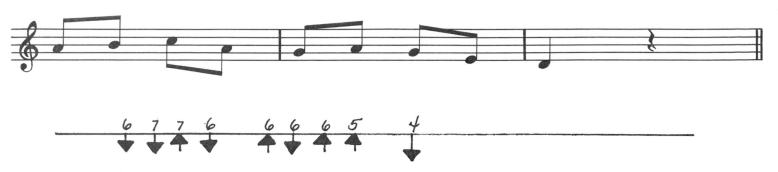

Another alternate version for last four measures:

photo Dave Whitson

HASTE TO THE WEDDING

Here's a Jig, in 6/8 time. To get an idea about how the rhythm goes count ONE two three FOUR five six very rapidly. This is a good tune in that it doesn't have to be played fast to sound good. Old time fiddler Dewey Dowell calls it the *King's March*.

HASTE TO THE WEDDING
"Adapted and Arranged By George Heaps - Nelson,"

SOLDIER'S JOY

This is a favorite among fiddlers and banjo players. Versions vary tremendously so again be ready to compromise. A variant title I have heard is the *King's Head*.

Chubby Anthony - Florida Bluegrass and Old Time Championship, 1974
Photo by Bob McClintock

SOLDIERS JOY

Adapted and Arranged By George Heaps - Nelson

Old Rusty Hay Bailer
Photo by Dave Whitsen

GARY OWEN

Another Jig. Notice how the first little phrase is simply a descending C major scale. *Gary Owen* was (and is) the theme song of the famed Seventh Cavalry, which ran into trouble on the Little Big Horn some years back and which now is a helicopter outfit.

GARY OWEN

Adapted and Arranged By George Heaps - Nelson

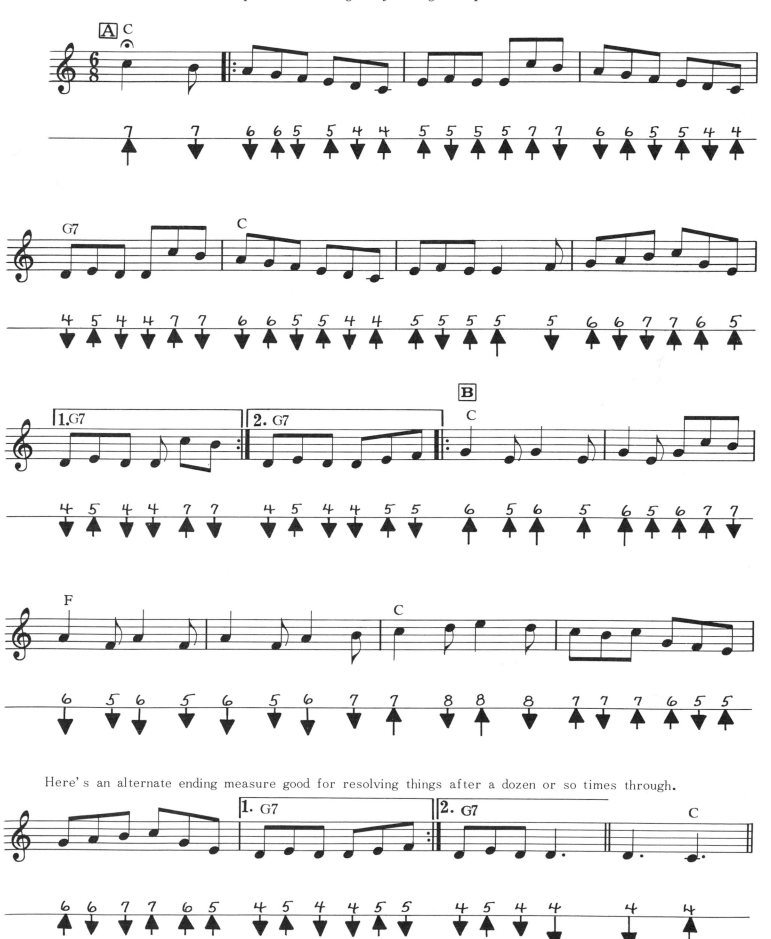

Here's an alternate ending measure good for resolving things after a dozen or so times through.

Farm in Virginia, 1940
Photo by A. Rothstein, Library of Congress Collection

Barn
Photo by Dave Whitsen

YEAR OF JUBILO

This one is generally associated with the Emancipation of 1863. The tune sounds like it could be older, perhaps of British origin like the preceding tunes, but the Afro-American influence is present in the very emphatic rhythm most musicians use on this piece. Maybe you could use the staccato chord technique described with the song *Round The Bend*.

YEAR OF JUBILO

Adapted and Arranged By George Heaps - Nelson

SALLY GOODIN'

Adapted and Arranged By George Heaps - Nelson

Folk Singer
Photo by Randolph Vance
Library of Congress Collection

SALLY GOODIN'
and ARKANSAS TRAVELER

Sally Goodin' and *Arkansas Traveler* are both classic American Hoedowns. The whole range of string band instruments are appropriate here and the tunes can stand some pretty rough treatment.

Photo of Library of Congress Collection

ARKANSAS TRAVELER

Adapted and Arranged By George Heaps - Nelson

THE WILD HORSE
AT STONEY POINT

This tune, sometimes called the *Pigtown Fling* or the *Pigtown Hoedown*. is slightly more complicated than the previous ones because it has three parts rather than two and the second one is in A minor. No special technique is necessary for this, just follow the indicated notes and be very sure that you are playing precise single notes. If you get a bunch of unwanted notes in with the melody note, the effect is spoiled.

Photo by Alice Owens

WILD HORSE AT STONEY POINT

Adapted and Arranged By George Heaps - Nelson

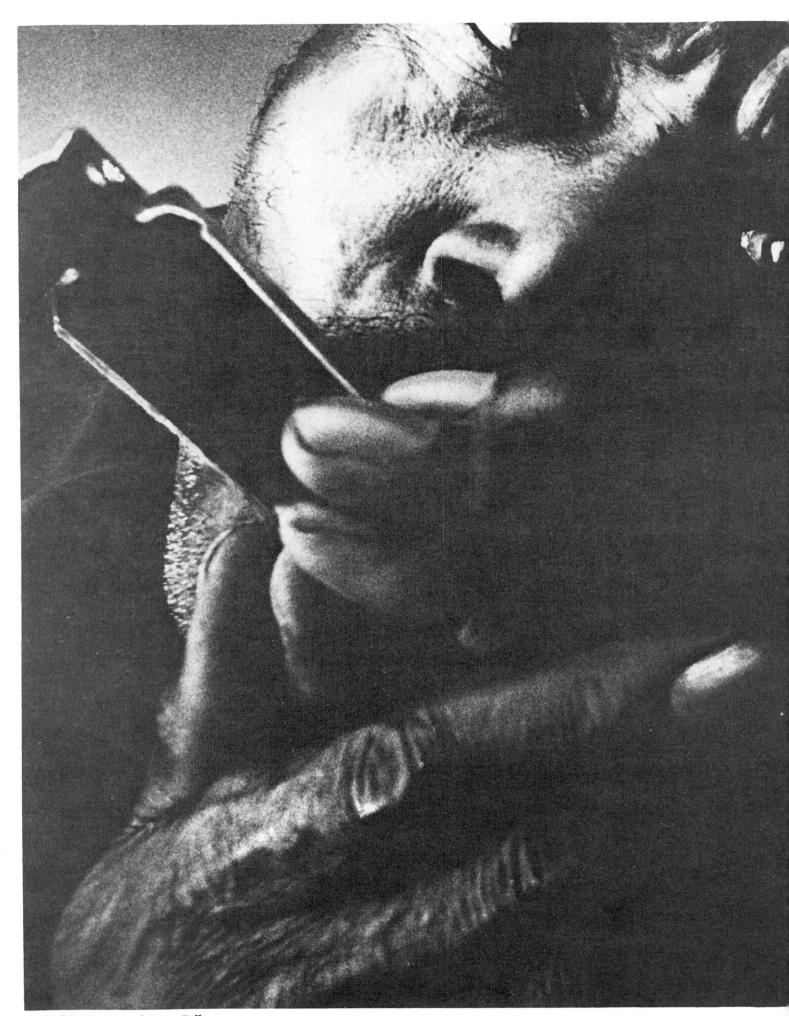

Big Walter Horton and Carey Bell
Photo by Peter Amft, Courtesy of Alligator Records

CHAPTER V
THE
BLUES

INTRODUCTION TO BLUES

Everything I've said about the necessity of listening a lot and not relying entirely on this or any other book needs to be re-emphasized when it come to blues. Luckily there is a lot of excellent blues harp on records. Listen to records, hear the music in person when possible, and then listen to records some more. There is a great deal of tasteless blues harp played by young white people who have little idea of the magnitude of the cultural leap they are making and who haven't spent nearly enough time absorbing and appreciating the music they are trying to play.

Whether you are more interested in Folk Blues à la Sonny Terry and Hammie Nixon, or the Big Chicago sound of people like Junior Wells and Little Walter or the "in between" players such as Sonny Boy Williamson I and Sonny Boy Williamson II, do yourself a favor and go to the source. Why tramp downstream for a drink of stirred up water when the clear spring is just as convenient?

Sorry if that was a bit heavy but it had to be said. The successful blues imitators have all gone to impeccably good places to learn their stuff and that is the main thing you can pick up from them, or from me for that matter. Maybe you'll be ultra successful at making yourself a part of this music, as John Hammond, Jr. or Charlie Musselwhite have done, maybe not. In any event you may get a lot of satisfaction out of it. All this preachin' at you was so you'll make better music, not out of fear that you could hurt the blues in any way; they were doing all right when you were still singing along with Mitch or screaming along with the Beatles or whatever you were doing before you wised up and bought a harmonica. Well, let's get to it before I get in the notion of taking up a collection.

GETTING THE IDEA OF CROSS HARP

So far you have been playing forwards or "straight" harp. Blues harp is usually played backwards — that's right backwards. Your "do" or tonic note is in number 2 hole draw rather than number 4 hole blow. On a C harmonica you wind up playing in G. (For the cross harp keys for various harmonicas see Appendix II.) From hole 2 draw to hole 5 draw we have a gapped G scale containing the notes GBCDEFG. When you learn to bend notes a little later on you can close the gaps. The F♮ rather than F# really sounds nice sometimes so don't let that throw you.

This backwards harp style is known as "cross" harp. To get an idea of what cross harp is like try this simple boogie. There is nothing here that you can't do with the technique you already have. Try it, it should not be too hard to figure out. For the sake of convenience the cross harp music is notated an octave high. Thus 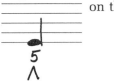 on the

preceding songs would be ⸻ in cross cross harp notation.

Graffitto
Photo by Marcus Johnson

BOOGIE

Adapted and Arranged By George Heaps - Nelson

Harp C
Key of G

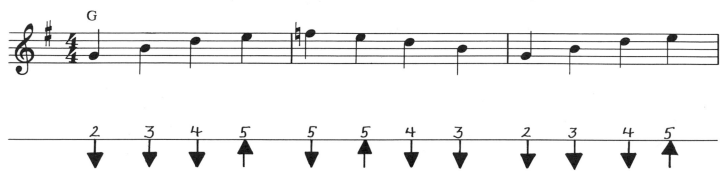

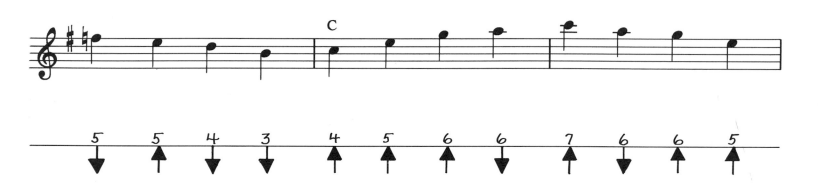

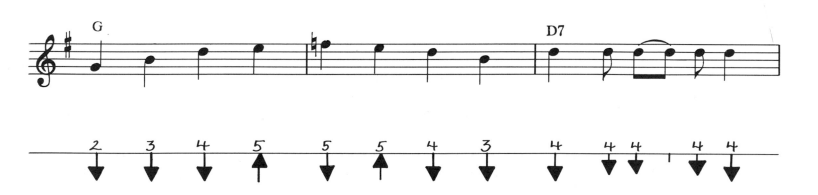

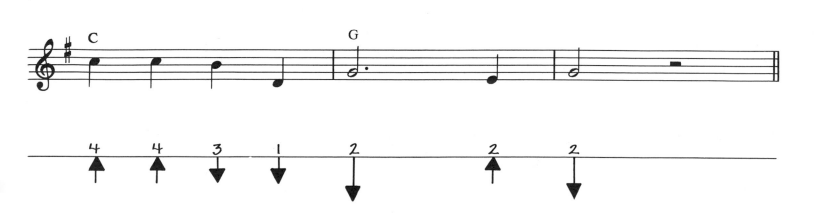

Here's *John Henry*, a well known Afro-American folk ballad that is again playable with no special technique.

JOHN HENRY

"Adapted and Arranged By George Heaps - Nelson,"

Harp C
Key of G

Cross Harp

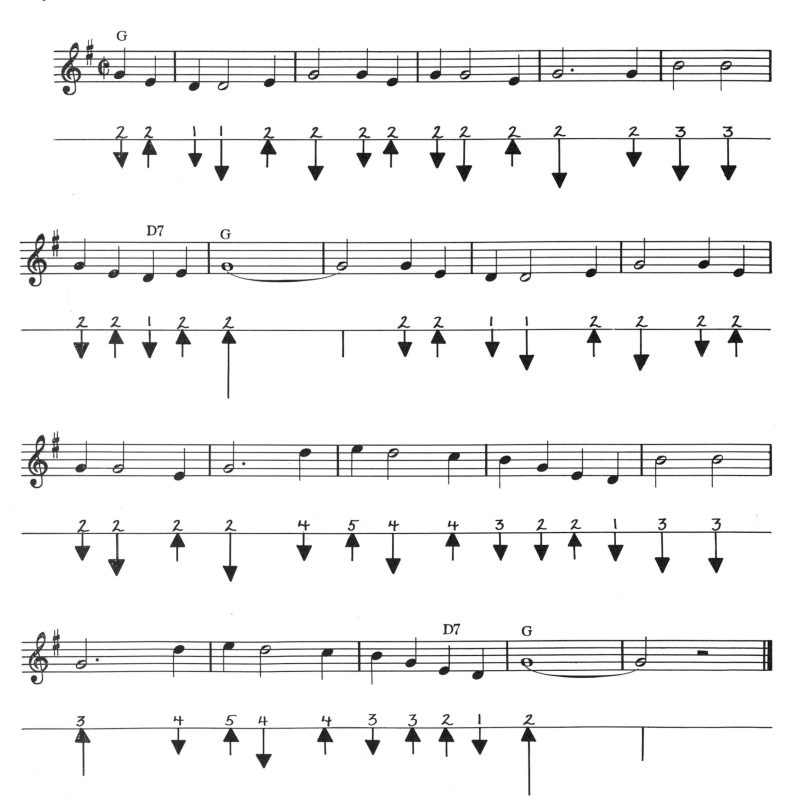

Little Walter
Photo Courtesy Chess/Janus Records

BENDING NOTES

Now that you have some notion of what is going on, and assuming that you are listening to some good records (see Discography), let's move on to bending notes. Bent notes are those beautiful slurs you hear where A, let's say slowly raises to a B, or a G lowers to F#. Bent notes are useful for filling the gaps in the 10 hole harps' blues scale. They are also quite useful for playing the "blue" notes which are slightly flatted third and seventh notes of the scale. In the case of G these notes are B-Bb and F#-F. The technique of bending notes is not really very hard. In fact I've never heard of anyone who really tried to learn who wasn't soon bending with the best of them. "Bend" is a good word here for the air column actually passes the reed at an angle. Bent notes are possible in both draw and blow situations. The bent draw note is the more important as drawn bending is most practical on the lower half of the harp, while bent blow notes aren't really possible down there. To make a bent draw note use the pursed lips method to get a single tone out of hole 3. Now drop your jaw and tongue and bring a lot of pressure to bear on that reed. Draw hard. Yes, it's hard on the reed, but that's how notes are bent.*

When you shift from a "bent" to an "unbent" note in the same hole you can think in terms of an ah-oo change. Your dentist has you say ah because when you do, you drop your jaw — oooo on the other hand approximates an ordinary pursed lips position for playing the natural note of the reed. The blown bent note is similarly formed though the jaw drop is less prominent. Try it on hole 7 or 8. Blow hard.

My own favorite, the Golden Melody is really a little stiff for blues playing — the Marine Band and Blues Harp are both very good choices here.

Most blues players do in fact use the pursed lips method for getting a single note, but it is possible to get a good bent note by the tongue blocking method. Why it works I'm not at all sure, but if you cover up part of the one open hole and draw hard, you can get your bends. Another way of making the bend is to turn the harp slightly downward into your lips. Draw, and again the air passes the reed at an angle, producing the desired effect. This really is rather unhandy for me in actual playing, though it may help you some.

A good reason for not using the tongue blocking method for blues is that there are other better things for the tongue to be doing. For instance, take one long draw breath on hole 2 or 3. Wiggle your tongue around in various ways and listen to the variety of tonal and punctuational effects you can get. Especially nice is a dit dit dit motion, which you can cut off air to the harp, enabling you to play a series of staccato notes with one breath. This builds the tension much better than a series of short breaths. Here's a little harp bit that I give to you for three reasons:

A. It contains bent notes.

B. It lets you use the dit dit tongue techniques for getting many short notes out of one long breath.

C. It employs the standard 12 bar blues pattern, about which I'll have more to say later.

I'm also giving you here the old time jazz spiritual *When the Saints Go Marchin' In*. There's a pretty radical bend here, from B down to A on the 3rd hole. That's a whole tone — you'll have to work to get it.

TONGUE TAPPING BLUES

Written By George Heaps - Nelson

Harp C
Key of G

Cross Harp

✳ Open your mouth and your lips to include holes 1 and 3.

WHEN THE SAINTS GO MARCHIN' IN

Adapted and Arranged By George Heaps - Nelson

Harp C
Key of G

Cross Harp

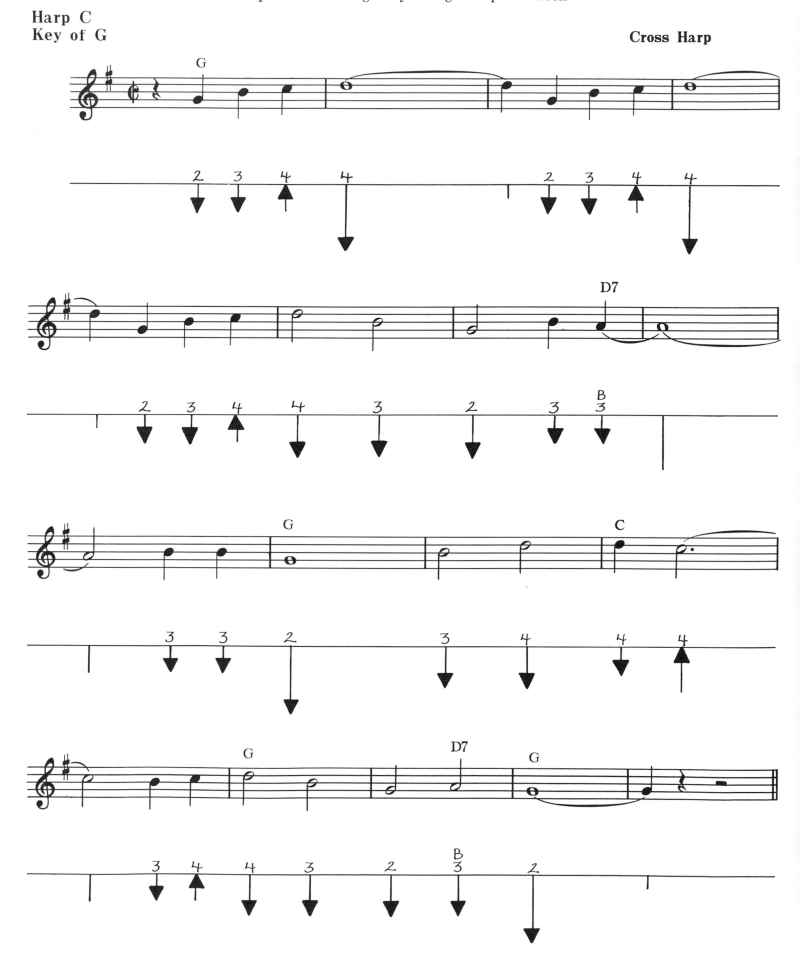

Old Cemetery
Photo by Dave Whitsen

RIFFS

Now before I get into the business of blues structure, here are some good riffs to play around with. Some hand techniques that can help these riffs include two new types of vibrato. The first is done by holding the harp between the thumb and the forefinger of the left hand and rather violently slapping the backside of the harp with your right hand. This works best on the long mournful notes that are so popular in modern Chicago blues. This vibrato is slower, rougher and more pulsating than the sweet quick hand vibrato we used in the earlier sections. The other "vibrato like" effect is even rougher. It consists of rhythmically shaking the harp from side to side so hard that the main note being played alternates with the one next to it (either up or down).

Work on lip and tongue variations and experiment with tonality. Talk into your harp. Alternate single notes with chords. Open up your lips a little wider and try some of these riffs two notes at a time. (Try to avoid breathiness however, one of the faults most prevalent among beginning blues harp players.) Make sure your breath is going through the harp — not whistling audibly over and around it. The one exception to this is that when you have a lungful of air and a chance to play a blow note you can expel some air through your nose. Keep your lips firm and tight though, and your music will be a lot clearer.

Charles S. Bush, Jr., Gainesville, Florida
Photo by Bob McClintock

RIFF NO. 1

Harp C
Key of G

Cross Harp

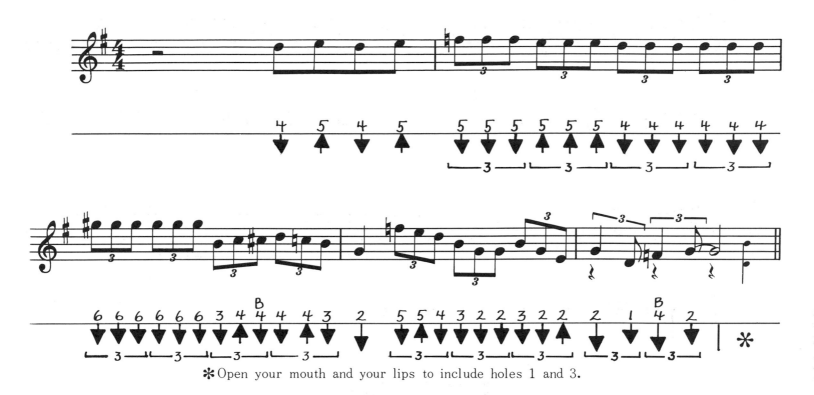

✱ Open your mouth and your lips to include holes 1 and 3.

RIFF NO. 2

Harp C
Key of G

Cross Harp

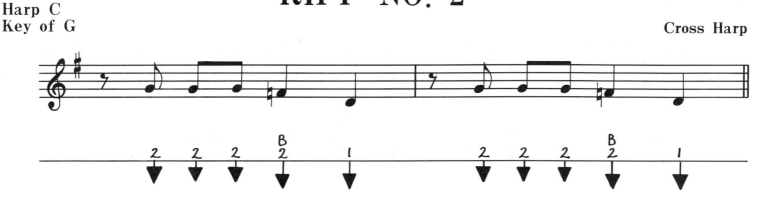

RIFF NO. 3

Harp C
Key of G

Cross Harp

RIFF NO. 4

Harp C
Key of G

Cross Harp

RIFF NO. 5

Harp C
Key of G

Cross Harp

RIFF NO. 6

Harp C
Key of G

Cross Harp

RIFF NO. 7

Harp C
Key of G

Cross Harp

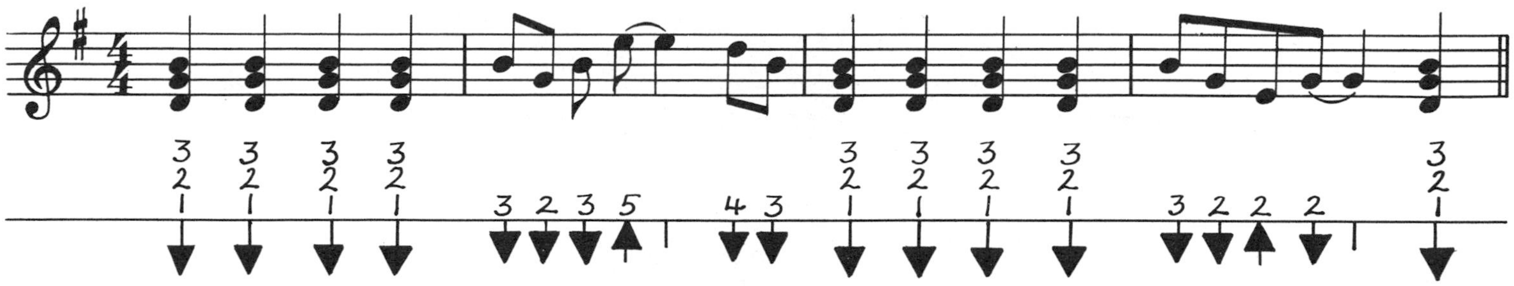

RIFF NO. 8

Harp C
Key of C

Straight Harp

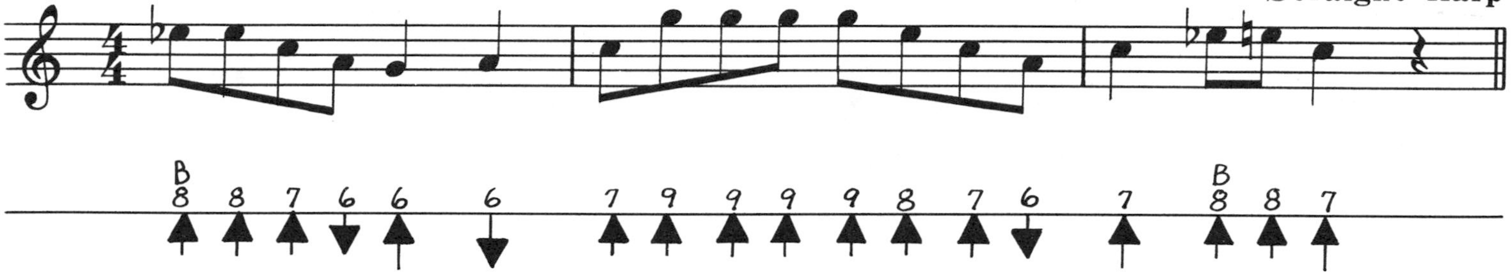

RIFF NO. 9

Harp C
Key of G

Cross Harp

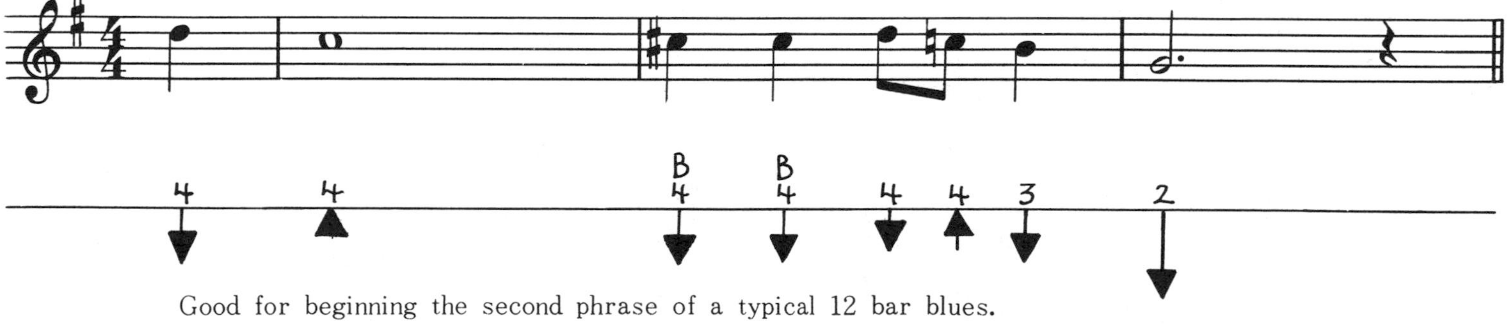

Good for beginning the second phrase of a typical 12 bar blues.

RIFF NO. 10

Harp C
Key of G

Cross Harp

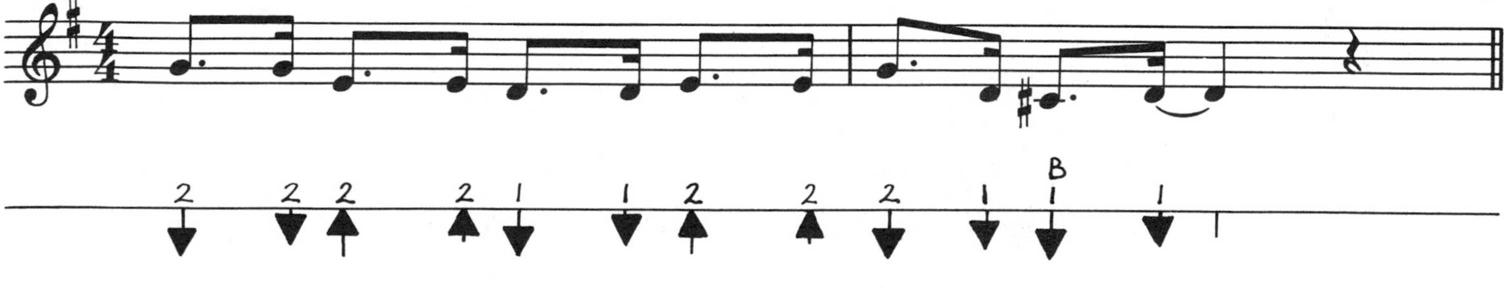

Good for ending a 12 bar blues.

Shed - Iowa, 1936
Photo by R. Lee, Library of Congress Collection

BLUES STRUCTURE

The techniques you've been working on are not extremely difficult. There are some good blues singers who use the harp as a nice afterthought sort of thing and who get by with not-too-much technique at all. Most of these guys have a firm grip on what blues music is about and a good idea of what notes not to play. There are also many enthusiastic novices to blues who master the bent note technique rapidly, learn a few runs and then proceed to sit in with anyone who'll let them — wailing away with little or no heed for the chord changes in the song and leaving no holes unfilled with harmonica music. Please don't do that and, if you do, don't tell anyone that you learned from this book.

So that you will have some notion of how to use the stuff you've got, I'm going to talk about blues structure for awhile. There are several basic blues patterns that include most of the music you'll hear bluesmen play.

TWELVE BAR BLUES

We'll begin with the standard three line twelve bar blues. Listen to any of your blues records for a few cuts and you'll hear a three-line song pattern something like this:

I got the blues so bad it hurts my feet to walk.

I got the blues so bad it hurts my feet to walk.

I got the blues so bad it hurts my tongue to talk.

Each of these lines takes up three bars (measures) of music and there are three on bar holes, one after each line. (In actual practice: sometimes the lines are longer and breaks shorter or vice versa.) These holes are usually filled by instrumental breaks such as the riffs you have learned. Most American folk music, the blues included, uses a three-chord accompaniment structure. These three chords have for their main notes the first, fourth and fifth notes of the scale. In the key of G, they are G, C and D. "Wait a minute," you screech, "I'm not playing a chord instrument like the guitar." Relax. Knowing this will make you a better blues musician. In most twelve bar blues the chords are used like this:

I GOT THE BLUES

G
I got the blues so bad it hurts my feet to walk
(Break if you know how.)
            C   G
I got the blues so bad it hurts my feet to walk
(Break.)
           D   C   G
I got the blues so bad it hurts my tongue to talk
(Break, Riff 10 is good here.)

Thus for a super simple but appropriate harp accompaniment — all you'd really need to know would be where to get notes that go with the song's chord structure. Here's a little diagram showing good solid holes to wail in for the 1, 4 and 5 chords on any diatonic ten hole harp. (For what keys go with what harps consult Appendix II.)

DIAGRAM

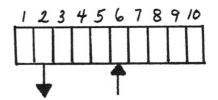

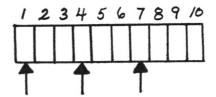

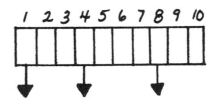

Turn back to the simple blues I gave you for note bending and tongue staccato. Play it again a few times. Everything I've said since I started in about the twelve bar blues is right there. *Frankie's Blues* is an old twelve bar blues that should be fairly easy to play.

FRANKIE'S BLUES

Adapted and Arranged By George Heaps - Nelson

Harp C
Key of G

Cross Harp

Now try *George's Blues*. The first version is a melody solo, the second is an accompaniment. Notice that the backup version is sparser and more subdued. It makes for a more interesting whole when the singer and his backup men aren't competing for glory.

Always keep working on varying and personalizing your tonality. No two harp players sound exactly alike (with the possible exception of Sonny Terry and his nephew J.C. Burris) so find your own way of using your lips, tongue, hands and mouth cavity, and you'll have your own sound.

GEORGE'S BLUES I

Adapted and Arranged By George Heaps - Nelson

Harp C
Key of G

Cross Harp

GEORGE'S BLUE'S II

Adapted and Arranged By George Heaps - Nelson

Harp C
Key of G

Cross Harp

Sonny Terry
Photo Courtesy M. Hohner Co.

The twelve bar blues form has some interesting variations, the most important of which is the verse chorus pattern.

Many country and rock tunes use this form. Hank William's *Move It On Over* and Little Richard's *Long Tall Sally* come to mind here.

In this form, a short verse is crowded into the first four bars and the final eight are used as a more relaxed two line chorus. If you take the *Blues So Bad* verse I used earlier and change it to the verse chorus pattern, it comes out like this:

Verse — Got the blues so bad
        hurts my feet to walk,
        Got the blues so bad
        it hurts my tongue to talk

Chorus — Got the blues so bad it hurts my feet to walk,
        I got the blues so bad it hurts my tongue to talk.

This type of song can be either fast or slow. Here's one of each for you to try:

A NICKEL IS A NICKEL

Adapted and Arranged By George Heaps - Nelson

Harp C
Key of G

Cross Harp

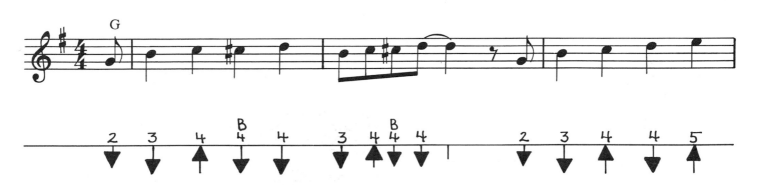

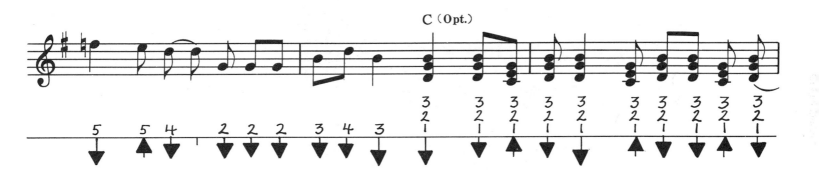

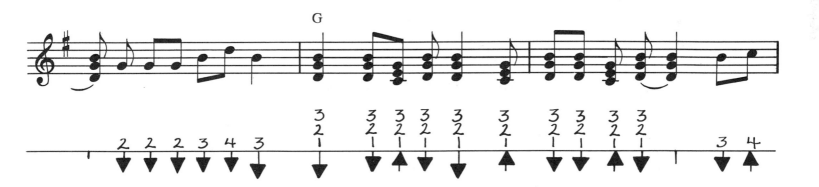

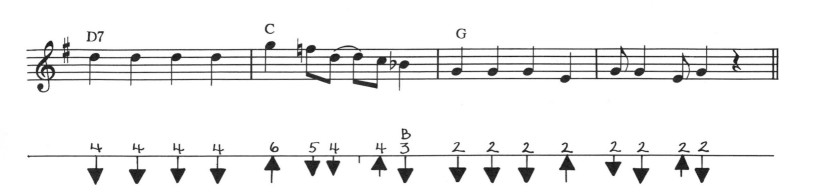

Standing the Ravages of Time
Photo by Dave Whitsen

EARLY IN THE MORNIN'

Adapted and Arranged By George Heaps - Nelson

Harp C
Key of G

Cross Harp

Old Cotton Fields Back Home
Photo by Dave Whitsen

Oh the Times When I Was Young
Photo by Dave Whitsen

EIGHT BAR BLUES

Another blues form is the 8 bar blues. *Trouble In Mind, Keys To the Highway, East St. Louis Blues, Stagolee,* and *Pistol Slapper Blues* all have a similar chord pattern. *Pistol Slapper Blues* is a good one for a starter.

PISTOL SLAPPER BLUES

Adapted and Arranged By George Heaps - Nelson

Harp C
Key of G

Cross Harp

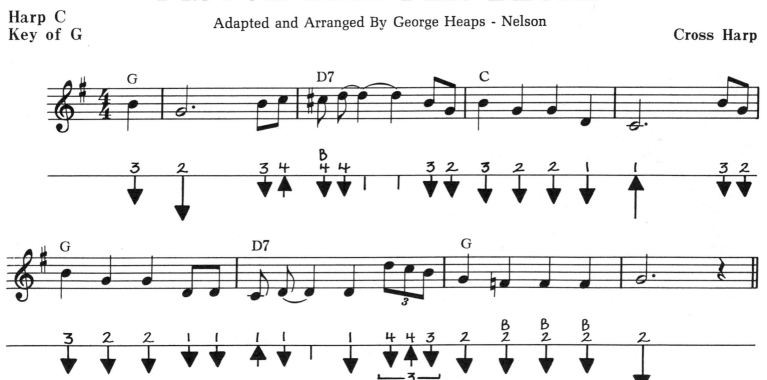

Another good blues of the eight bar type is
Hurtin' Blues.

HURTIN' BLUES

Adapted and Arranged By George Heaps - Nelson

Harp C
Key of G

Cross Harp

Kirke - Photo by Marcus Johnson

John Nelson Getting The Hang Of It
Photo by James A. Nelson

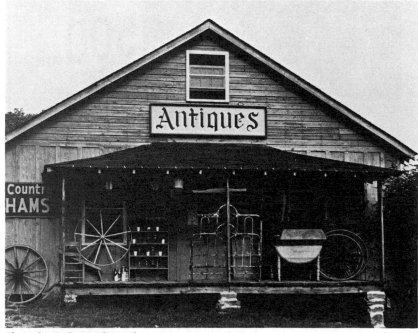

Photo by Bob McClintock

Wisconsin Farm, 1937
Photo by R. Lee
Library of Congress Collection

Another eight bar blues you should probably look up is *Goin To Germany*. This song was played years ago by Cannons Jug Stompers with Noah Lewis on harmonica. You can hear them play it on Origin Jazz Library No. 4. No two verses are played alike and there are a couple of ten bar verses in the middle there. Goin' To Germany also became a favorite of jug bands during the 1960's often in more regular and less interesting versions. Unfortunately we couldn't include a version here because of copyright hassles. Maybe you'd like to try it in straight — or "forward" style. Lewis himself played it cross harp — but straight harp, usually with lots of flutters and bent blow notes, is a common jug band style. Even some later bluesmen have played that way. On Blues Classics 21, Sonny Boy Williamson plays straight harp for *Baby Please Don't Go* and *Stack of Dollars*. Jimmy Reed plays straight harp often, too. If you want to do *Goin' To Germany* as a duet, give the straight player a G harp and the cross man a C.

Outside Berlin
Photo by Hermann Harz

Railroad Station - Bell, Florida
Photo by Alice Owens

South End of Amish Cow
Photo by Marcus Johnson

CHAPTER VI - ETC.

SPECIAL TYPES OF HARPS
SOLO TUNED HARPS

If you have been playing much fiddle tune harp, you will have noticed that the typical Marine Band tuning has its limitations. Sometimes you grope for that missing low F or A. If that is the case then some type of solo tuned harp might be just what you're looking for. The Marine Band soloist is no longer made as of 1975 but you might find one in a store somewhere. The larger twelve hole Marine Band can be procured in *solo tuning* by special order (C only), and both Hohner and Kratt make nice 12 hole 3 octave chromatics which will certainly do the trick. These 12 hole harps are usually tuned like this.

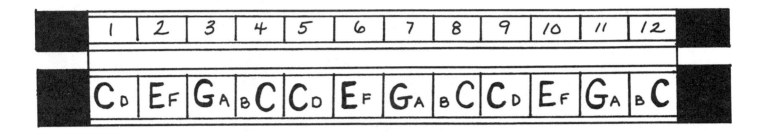

Here are two fiddle tunes that are impossible on the standard 10 hole Marine Band but playable on a solo tuned harmonica.

Harness on Wall
Photo by Alice Owens

ROSIN THE BEAU

Rosin the Beau is a slow fiddle piece that was
used for many political songs in the 19th century.
It is probably the parent tune of *Down in the
Willow Garden (Rose Connally)*, a widely sung
southern murder ballad.

ROSIN THE BEAU

Adapted and Arranged By George Heaps - Nelson,

Soloist

THE GAL I LEFT BEHIND ME

The Gal I Left Behind Me is an old Scottish tune with several sets of verses. I first heard my older brothers singing and playing it with the cowboy words: "I struck the trail in seveny-nine with the herd strung out behind me . . ."

THE GAL I LEFT BEHIND ME

Adapted and Arranged By George Heaps - Nelson

Soloist

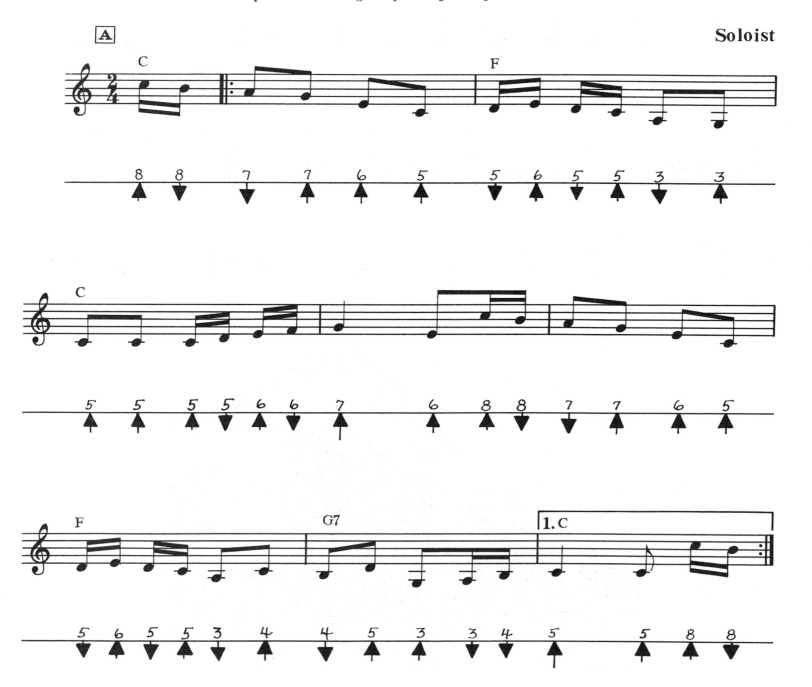

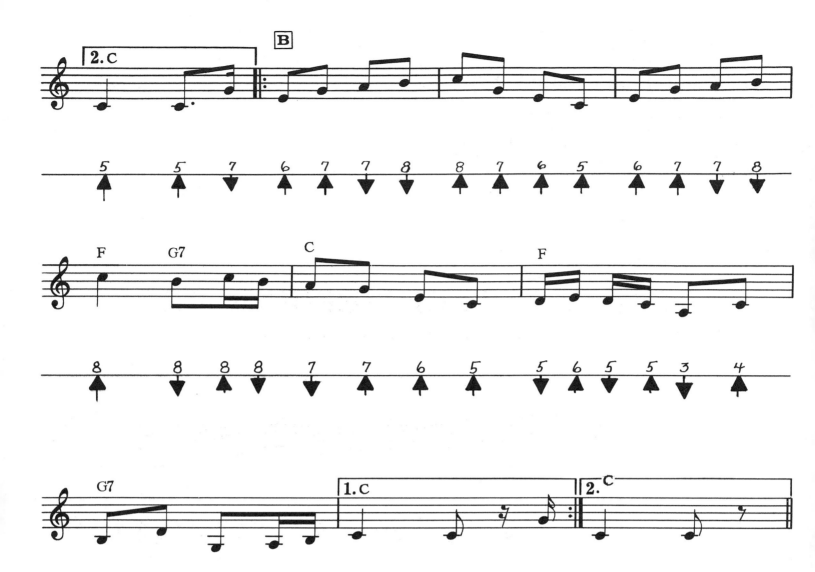

Ohio, 1938
Photo by B. Shahn, Library of Congress Collection

THE CHORDOMONICA

The Chordomonica is a newly invented harmonica that makes a good stab at resolving the problem of discords while giving you full scales to work with. It is two harmonicas together, equipped with a slide-button arrangement that allows only one of the harps to sound at a time. In that respect it's like a chromatic harp, but the similarity ends there. Here are two diagrams, the first is of "button out" position and the second gives the notes that sound when the button is pushed.

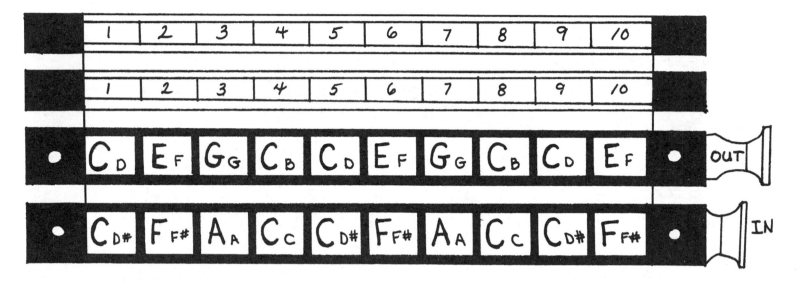

Essentially this harp has four full chords: button out blow is C; button out draw is G7; button in blow is F; and button in draw is C diminished. In this way you are not held to one chord for a given note. C is available in C, F and C diminished chords; F in G7 and F chords; A in F and C diminished; G in G and C.

It takes some getting used to, for even the simplest scale forces you to make use of the button (A is unavailable in the button out position). The inventor of this harmonica, Cham-Ber Huang, is to be congratulated for an ingenious idea. Since there are no discords, lip technique is not important. I rarely play single tones on my chordomonica. I prefer the rich sounds of chords, letting the top note carry the melody and the lower ones harmonize.

See if *Bury Me Beneath the Willow* gives you some idea as to how you can use the chordomonica.

Requiescat in Pace
Photo by Bob McClintock

BURY ME BENEATH THE WILLOW

Adapted and Arranged By George Heaps - Nelson

Chordomoica

If you're confused but intrigued, Cham-Ber Huang has written a book describing how to play the chordomonica. A more complicated model, the Chordomonica II also exists. It's got two slides and two more chords, A minor and D minor seventh.

Turkey on Georgia Farm
Photo by Bob McClintock

Woman Fishing
Photo by Alice Owens

MINOR HARPS

Hohner now makes a 10 hole 20 reed minor harp which can be an interesting addition to your harmonica collection. It is set up as follows,- assuming that the one we're looking at is in C.

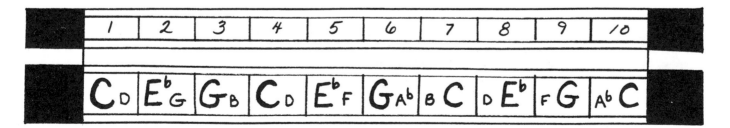

There are certain limitations on what this type of harp can do, because a lot of the American Folk Songs you think of as minor actually have major strains. The second difficulty is that B natural. If it were Bb there'd be a pile of playable minor folk songs but since it isn't we've got to do the best we can. Here's an approximation of *Drill Ye Tarriers*.

DRILL YE TARRIERS

Harp C minor

OTHER HARPS

In addition to the common 10 hole, the Soloist, the minor harp and the Chordomonica, there are several other types of diatonic harmonicas that are useful to the folk musician.

First, there are the extended Marine Bands which are simply larger versions of what we've been using. They retain the "gapped" tuning that makes cross harp possible but they are 12 and 14 hole instruments. Hohner makes them in C and G. The C versions have some notes that are lower than the ordinary C with 10 holes, while the G adds notes on the higher end. I have found these instruments a little awkward. They are too large to get my hands around and the reeds seem a little stiff in the G harps' upper register. The C harp with its low tones makes a nice instrument for backing up someone else however, and you might want to try one.

Another category is the octave tuned harp. Of these the most common and useful are the "concert" jobs that have 40 reeds and 10 double holes. They're slightly larger than the ordinary 10 hole and have wider holes. Essentially they consist of two harmonicas, one on the top of the other and tuned an octave apart. When you blow on the number 4 hole, for instance, you hear 2 C's rather than one.

As you may have surmised, that makes a louder fuller sound. It also makes the instrument slightly more inflexible. Bent notes are, for all practical purposes impossible. The wider holes make them nice harps if you have lots of trouble getting good clear tones on the smaller harps.

There are three very good 10 hole 40 reed models available. Hohner makes two, the Marine Band Full Concert and the Auto Valve (the latter is

Photo Courtesy M. Hohner Co.

famous among older players as an easy blowing instrument) and Kratt makes one, the Concert Warbler.

Some other octave tuned harps I've seen used are the Comet, the El Centenario, made by Hohner, and the Bandmaster Octave Harmonica. Don't be fooled by the apparently large numbers of holes on these last three instruments. In terms of actual playing range four holes on one of these equals one hole on the standard model.

To show this graphically☐on a normal 10 hole 20 reed harp =⊞ on one of the harps mentioned above.

The Comet comes in various sizes and shapes including a two sided model (one side C, the other

Photo Courtesy M. Hohner Co.

G). It has the advantage of a plastic comb. I also like the slightly curved playing surface. El Centenario commemorated the first century of Mexican independence (1810-1910). It is in a two octave tuning i.e. when you play you hear notes two octaves apart. In range it is the equivalent of an 8 hole C harmonica. It's billed as good for Latin American songs but its special full sounds makes it also nice for polkas and other various types of dance music.

The Bandmaster Octave harmonicas are nice sounding inexpensive alternatives to Hohners, they are a very reasonable buy. They come in two sided models in C and G. Both the Comet and the Bandmaster Octave harmonicas come in various lengths. The longer ones, though more expensive, are well worth the price differential because of their increased playing range.

Tremolo harmonicas are similar in appearance to the octave tuned harps but rather than being tuned an octave apart, the two sets of reeds are tuned ever so slightly at variance with one another. The conflicting vibrations that result make a pulsating quiver or tremolo.

Photo Courtesy M. Hohner Co.

The Hohner Echo series are undoubtly the best known harmonicas of this type while Bandmaster again provides an inexpensive second choice, the Bandmaster Tremolo Harmonica. These instruments come in a wide range of sizes and keys. Some are two sided (C and G, A and D, Bb and F) making the investment more reasonable. As with the octave harmonicas, four holes equals one hole on a ten hole harp for purposes of determining the playing range.

The tremolo harmonicas are without doubt the most popular "variety" harps. They have a sound that is pleasant, though the automatic quality of the tremolo bothers some. As with the other double reed types it is actually easier to get clear notes on a tremolo than on an ordinary single reed harp. This, combined with the tremolo effect make it possible for a player with poor lip technique and no tongue or hand technique to make pretty music. You can't deliver as personal a statement as with a standard ten hole, and cross harp is of course impossible, but if you can get by those objections — the tremolo is a nice harmonica to have around.

Photo Courtesy M. Hohner Co.

Blue Ridge Mountain Farm, 1937
Photo by J. Vachon, Library of Congress Collection

SPECIAL TECHNIQUES

PLAYING MINOR ON A MAJOR HARP

Another way of playing minor songs is to play in A minor on a 10 hole C major harmonica. There is a full octave of the natural A minor scale in holes 6 through 10 plus some nice lower notes in holes 4 and 5. The absence of an A in the bottom octave hurts but here again a Marine Band Soloist solves that problem. *When Johnny Comes Marchin' Home Again* is playable on the standard 10 hole.

Try *Nottamun Town*, *Ground Hog* and *O Come Emmanuel* that way too.

Washstand in Dog Run
Photo by W. Evans,
Library of Congress Collection

108

WHEN JOHNNY COMES MARCHIN' HOME

Adapted and Arranged By George Heaps - Nelson

Harp C
Key A minor

DOUBLE CROSS HARP
MOUNTAIN MODAL STYLE

Some old timey songs sound somewhere between major and minor. The scale they use is often called mountain modal. The educated types will tell you that you are playing in the Dorian mode. In simple terms, go from D (4↓) to the next higher D (8↓)on a C harmonica and you have the scale. I call this type of playing double cross harp. Try playing *Pretty Polly*.

PRETTY POLLY

Adapted and Arranged By George Heaps - Nelson

Harp C
Key D modal

Double Cross Harp

Some other ones you can play in this way are *Shady Grove*, the *House Carpenter* and *The Great High Wind That Blew The Low Post Down*. This last one is a wonderful tune that the late Bob Beers played on the fiddle. He recorded it on an album called "Dumbarton's Drums" (Columbia, now discontinued), perhaps you'll be lucky enough to find a copy somewhere.

Mower
Photo by Marcus Johnson

DOUBLE CROSS BLUES

Double cross harp can also be used for blues, but mainly for fill in playing rather than melody. Here are a couple of riffs to work on.

D isn't the only oddball blues key possibility on a C harp. One time Memphis Charlie Musselwhite told me he could play five keys on one harp. I suspect that these keys were C (straight harp), G (cross harp), D (double cross), E and A. In case you think I'm name dropping here I met the guy only once, he doesn't know me from Adam's off ox and it will do you absolutely no good to tell him George sent you.

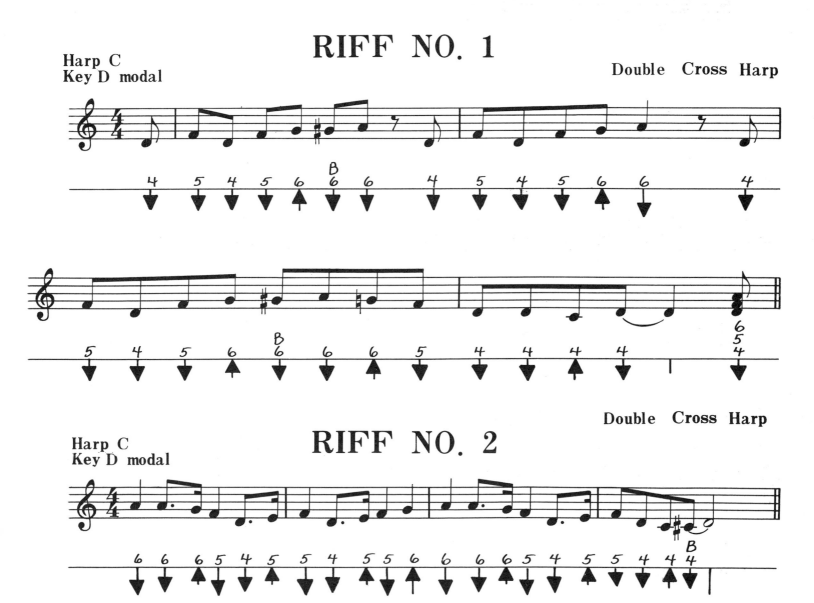

DOUBLE CROSS MINOR

Notice that the D to D modal scale DEFGABCD is only different from D minor in that it has a B natural rather than a B flat. If you can find minor songs that leave out this note you're all set to play in D minor.

Take a stab at *Poor Wayfaring Stranger.*

POOR WAYFARING STRANGER

Adapted and Arranged By George Heaps - Nelson

Harp C
Key D minor

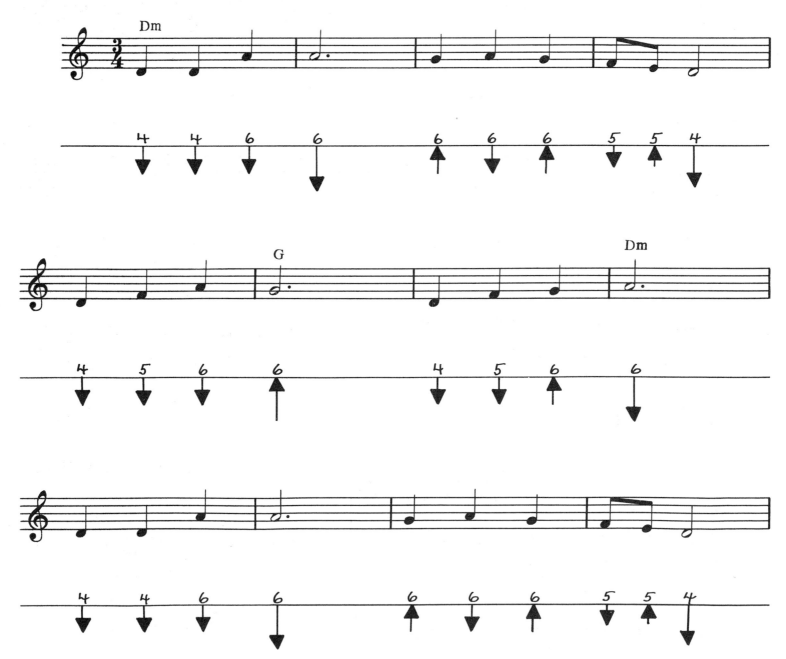

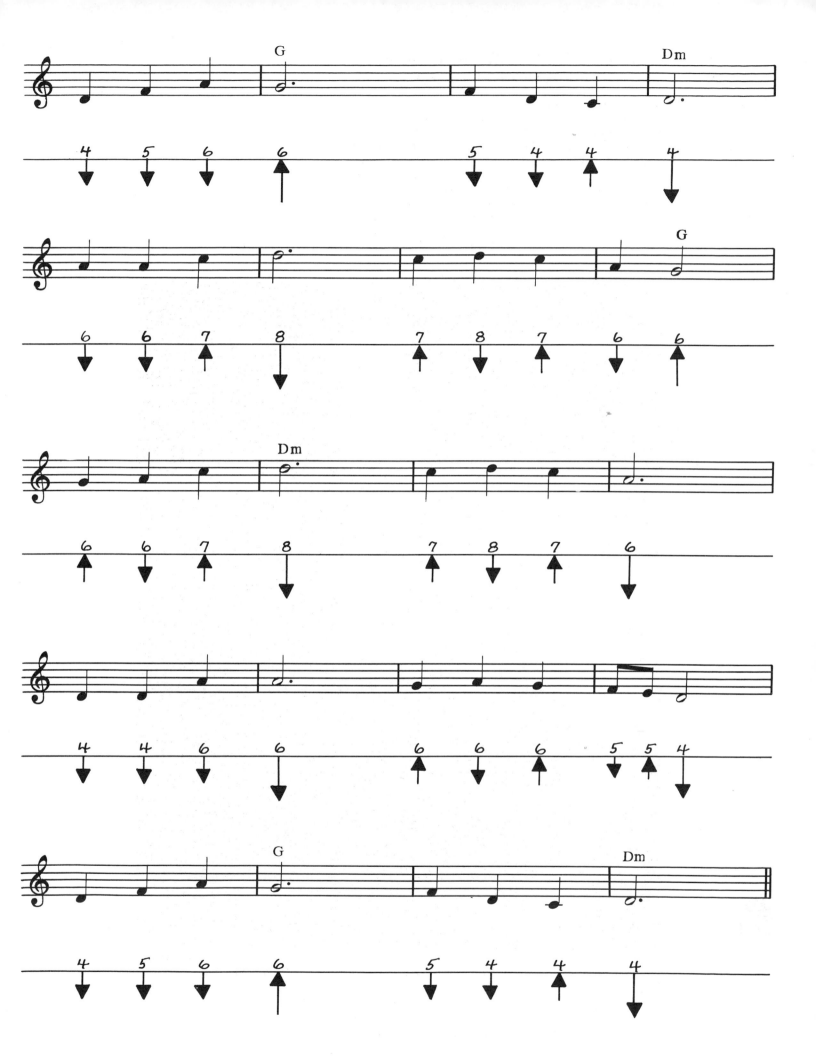

CROSS HARP FOR OLD TIME, COUNTRY AND BLUEGRASS

Using cross harp for old time, country and bluegrass is not terribly new. If you can find any old 78's by Deford Bailey or LP's with Red Parham you'll see what I mean. The most important recent player doing this is Charlie McCoy who has been working as a studio musician in Nashville for some time. Turn to your local country station and listen for awhile — you'll hear him. He's oriented more toward riffs and backup than a literal treatment of the tune, but he sure gets around on the harmonica.

Charlie McCoy
Photo Courtesy M. Hohner Co.

Use *Old Joe Clark* and *Do Lord* to get a notion of how cross harp can be useful in old time and country music. *Old Joe Clark* is also available one octave higher than the version I've indicated. Start on 8↓ and see if you can work it out yourself.

OLD JOE CLARK

Adapted and Arranged By George Heaps - Nelson

Harp C
Key of G

Cross Harp

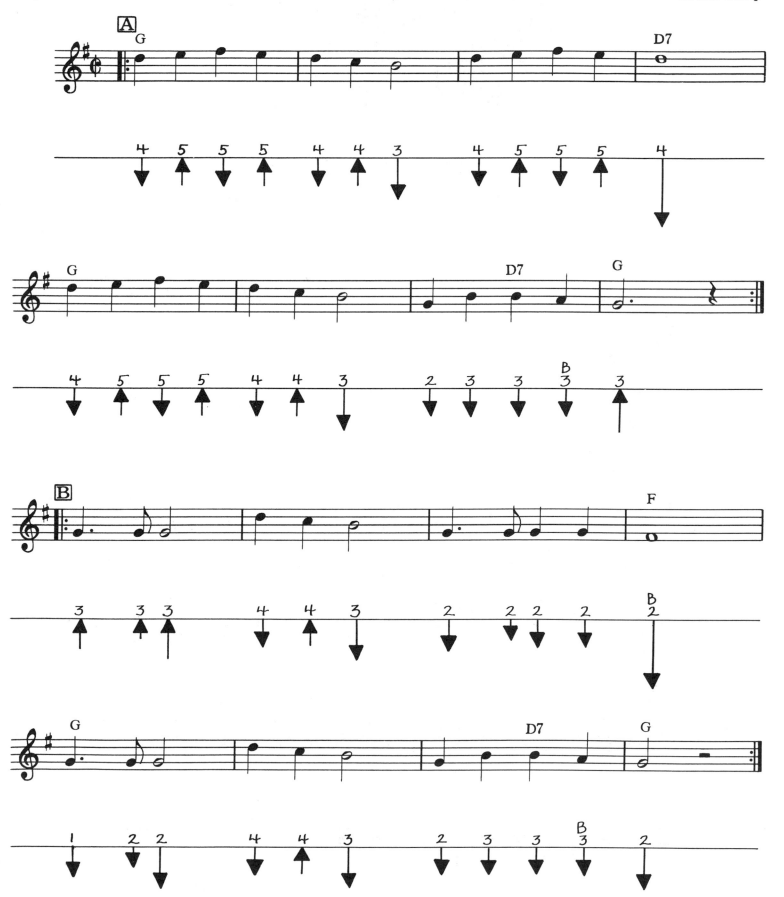

Rev. Dan Smith
Gospel Singer and Harmonica Player
Photo by Ann Meuer

DO LORD

"Adapted and Arranged By George Heaps - Nelson,"

Harp C
Key of G

Cross Harp

Photo by Alice Owens

STRAIGHT AND CROSS DUETS

When as a kid I first learned to play cross harp I started playing duets with my old friend George Keller.

He played straight harp and I played cross. We usually used one of the following four harp combinations:

Key of D — straight harp D — Cross G

Key of E — straight harp E — Cross A

Key of G — straight harp G — Cross C

Key of A — straight harp A — Cross D

As G is the lowest of the 12 harp keys available the first two combinations put the cross harp in a lower octave than the straight. In the second two combinations the two harps are pretty much in the same octave, for the low end of a C is comparable to the middle G range.

The very best kind of songs for this treatment are those in which black and white influences and styles are combined. We used to play *John Henry, Casey Jones, When the Saints Go Marchin' In, Columbus Stockade Blues, Brown's Ferry Blues, Gotta See Your Mama, Frankie and Johnny* and *Nashville Blues.* I think that *Goin' Down the Road Feelin' Bad* and *Crawdad Song* would be good that way too. Get a partner and try *Frankie and Johnny* cross and straight in the key of G.

George Keller, Cherokee, Iowa
Photo by Lillie Keller

FRANKIE AND JOHNNY

1st Harp (Straight) G
2nd Harp (Cross)   C

"Adapted and Arranged By George Heaps - Nelson,"

119

SELF-ACCOMPANIMENT — HOLDER VS. SLACK JAW

There are two or three good ways to accompany yourself on other instruments while playing the harp. Perhaps the simplest and most obvious is to hold the harp in your left hand while playing bones, washboard, piano or whatever else you want to play with the right.

A more elaborate and popular arrangement is a harmonica holder, sometimes purchased, often homemade. There are all sorts of homemade devices that can do just fine. My friend Mitch Johnson of Cherokee, Iowa made his out of a metal magazine rack while the late Carl Miller, also of Cherokee had a special welded rig of heavy steel that he used. Store bought holders come in two styles. The more popular ones are the around-the-neck jobs used by the great bluesman Dr. Isaiah Ross and many contemporary singer songwriter types. There is another kind that attaches to a guitar. J.D. Short used one, I believe, but they aren't too popular as they have marred up some guitars. The main advantage that the homemade ones have is that they usually don't let the harp go inching away from you as the manufactured around-the-neck ones have a tendency to do.

Arnold Keith Storm
Photo Courtesy Folk Legacy Records

Instruments I have seen played along with harps in holders include guitar, steel guitar, banjo, mandolin, banjo-mandolin, washboard, piano, accordion, uke, concertina, and autoharp. There's no reason a good armpit fiddler couldn't play a duet with himself on the harp though I've yet to see that done.

If you get into the one-man-band routine you can always play something with your feet, such as bass drum, hi hat cymbal and various homemade bass and washbord contraptions. I even heard of a guy who played harmonica with his mouth, guitar with his hands and steel guitar with his feet. Supposedly the steel was hooked to a roller skate and the guy strummed it with his big toe on which he had placed a thumb (toe?) pick. I only about half believed the story.

George With Harp In Mouth
Photo by Bob McClintock

If you really want to amaze your friend, throw away that holder, shove the left end of your harp into the left side of your mouth and try to play a simple tune with no hands. If you have been using the tongue blocking method for obtaining single notes it shouldn't be too hard — soon you'll learn to move the harp with your lips and tongue. Though you probably won't ever get much higher than hole 8, many songs are possible within the range at your disposal. This no hands style is best accomplished with a Vest Pocket Harp or Old Standby from Hohner or a Kratt Mel-o-dee. With that we'll leave you.

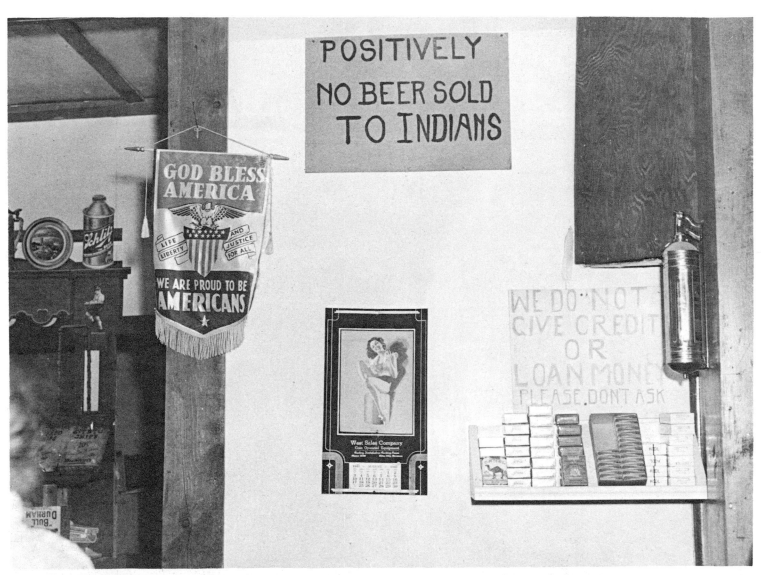

Bar-Birney, Montana, 1941
Photo by Post-Wolcott, Library of Congress Collection

Mountain Cabin-Kentucky, 1940
Photo by Post-Wolcott, Library of Congress Collection

Waterfall-North Georgia
Photo by Bob McClintock

Antiques in Newberry, Florida
Photo by Alice Owens

122

APPENDIX I.

EVERYTHING
YOU ALWAYS WANTED
TO KNOW
ABOUT MUSIC*

*BUT WERE AFRAID TO ASK

The music reading skills necessary for using the notation in this book are minimal. The staff has five lines and four spaces which are named as follows:

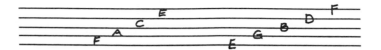

They are often remembered by using the insipid mnemonic devices FACE (for spaces) and Every Good Boy Does Fine (for lines). If you wish to think from the top down rather than the bottom up you could substitute Evil Cannot Always Fail (for spaces) and Frantically Delbert Bit Gerald's Ear (for lines).

Some lines and spaces above and below the staff (ledger lines) are used in this book — they are as follows:

To connect these various markings with the reality of your harp — refer back to the "C" harp and Cross Harp charts.

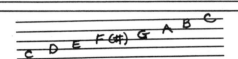 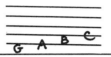

The fraction-like expressions that you see at the beginning of each piece are known as time signatures.

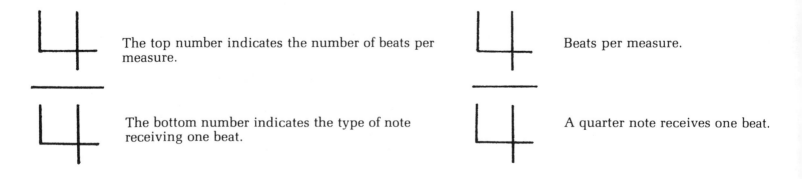

The top number indicates the number of beats per measure.

Beats per measure.

The bottom number indicates the type of note receiving one beat.

A quarter note receives one beat.

Means 4/4 or common time.

Means 2/2 or common time cut in half.

The basic kinds of notes you have to choose from are represented as follows:

The note values above are for 4/4 or common time. If you were playing in 6/8 time the note values would change.

Note that each of these types of note is sustained twice as long as the preceding one (going from left to right). A dot beside a note makes that note one and one half times as longs as it ordinarily would be and a tie ♩♩ means that the second note is essentially an unbroken continuation of the first.

Measures are separated from each other by
vertical bars.

The time signatures used in this book are: 𝄵
or 2/2, or cut time; 3/4, or waltz time; 4/4, or
common time; 2/4, usually distinguishable in folk
music from 4/4 by being a little livelier; and 6/8
time, which has two types, jig time and a slower
march style represented in this collection by *When
Johnny Comes Marchin' Home*. Here are some
simpler measures from each of these times with
counting patterns given below:

THE KEY SIGNATURE

The sharps # and the flats b given at the beginning of each piece indicate what notes are to be sharped and flatted throughout the song. It also tells us what key the song is in. All the songs in this book, *with the exception of the cross harp ones and the C minor song Drill Ye Tarriers,* are written with no sharps or flats which is the key of C. To help you know what is going on when you read music from other sources I have included a little table giving what key has how many sharps or flats (i.e. if you have one b — the key is F, one # the key is G).

NUMBER	FLATS	SHARPS
1	F	G
2	Bb	D
3	Eb	A
4	Ab	E
5	Db	B
6	Gb	F#

At 6 we come together; for our purposes, F# = Gb. For all keys the blow notes will be the first, third, fifth and eighth notes of the scale (do mi sol do) and the draw notes will be the second, fourth, sixth and seventh notes (re fa la ti). The exception to this is number two hole which is discussed in the text.

To make this clearer, here are some charts showing the blow and draw notes on the middle four holes (4-7) for several popular keys.

Machine Shed on Rented Farm, 1937
Photo by R. Lee, Library of Congress Collection

Small Town Upstate New York
Photo by Jim Lloyd

KEY OF C

BLOW NOTES
C E G C
4 5 6 7

DRAW NOTES
D F A B
4 5 6 7

KEY OF G

BLOW NOTES
G B D G
4 5 6 7

DRAW NOTES
A C E F#
4 5 6 7

KEY OF D

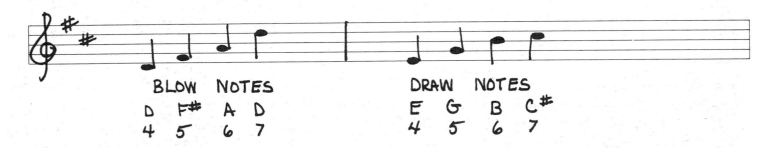

BLOW NOTES
D F# A D
4 5 6 7

DRAW NOTES
E G B C#
4 5 6 7

KEY OF A

BLOW NOTES
A C# E A
4 5 6 7

DRAW NOTES
B D F# G#
4 5 6 7

KEY OF F

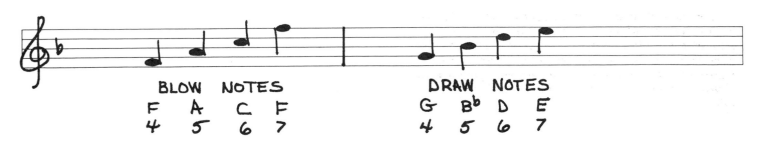

BLOW NOTES
F A C F
4 5 6 7

DRAW NOTES
G Bb D E
4 5 6 7

APPENDIX II.
HARPS, KEYS AND STYLES

Untitled
Photo by Bob McClintock

Here is a little series of charts to help you keep styles, harps and keys in mind. I am not including a chart on straight harp as I assume that if you are smart enough to read you are smart enough to figure out that if you want to play straight harp in C you use a C harp, in F# you use an F# harp etc. OK?

CROSS HARP

To use this chart decide upon the key you want to play in, find it in the left hand column and you will see the harp you need to use in the right hand column. Remember for our purposes C# =Db, D# = Eb, F# = Gb, G# = Ab, and A# = Bb.

KEY	HARP
C	F
C#	F#
D	G
Eb	Ab
E	A
F	Bb
F#	B
G	C
Ab	C#
A	D
Bb	Eb
B	E

DOUBLE CROSS

To find the right harp for the Mountain Modal or Double Cross minor key you have chosen find the key in the left column and the harp in the right one.

MOUNTAIN MODE* OR MINOR

KEY	HARP
C	Bb
C#	B
D	C
Eb	C#
E	D
F	Eb
F#	E
G	F
Ab	F#
A	G
Bb	Ab
B	A

*Dorian mode to the learned

NATURAL MINOR ON ON A MAJOR HARP

As with the cross harp chart find the key you want in the left hand column and the harp you need in the corresponding right hand one.

KEY	HARP
Cm	Eb
C#m	E
Dm	F
Ebm	F#
Em	G
Fm	Ab
F#m	A
Gm	Bb
Abm	B
Am	C
Bbm	C#
Bm	D

APPENDIX III.
DISCOGRAPHY

Chimney-Taccoa, Georgia
Photo by Bob McClintock

A & M SP 4379 — Sonny Terry and Brownie McGhee
ADELPHI 1007 — Furry Lewis. Bukka White. Gus Cannon
AHURA MAZDA 2003 — Harmonica Williams
ALLIGATOR AL 4702 — Big Walter Horton with Carey Bell
AMERICA 30AM 6136 — Willie Mabon (French import)
ARCHIVE OF FOLK FS 206 — Sonny Terry
    FS 242 — "Brownie and Sonny"
ARHOOLIE 1056 — Charlie Musselwhite
    1065 — "Dr. Ross — His First Recordings"

2005 — Guitar Slim and Jelly Belly
2009 — Jesse Fuller "Frisco Blues"
2020 — Sonny Boy Williamson
ATCO 33-389 — "Louisiana Red Sings The Blues"
ATLANTIC SD 1347 — "Blue Ridge Mountain Music"
    SD 1348 — "Roots Of The Blues"
    SD 1352 — "Blues Roll On"
    SD 8251 — John Hammond "Southern Fried"
BARRELHOUSE BH 04 — "Chicago Boogie"

BIOGRAPH 12028 — Larry Johnson "Country Blues"
    12036 — Dan Smith "God Is Not Dead"

BIRCH 1944 — "Mac and Bob" (Old time country music)

BLUE LABOR 101 — Sonny Terry

BLUES CLASSICS BC 2 — "Jug, Jook, and Washboard Bands"
    BC 3 — "Sonny Boy Williamson 1937-1942"
    BC 11 — Blind Boy Fuller with Sonny Terry
    BC 20 — "Sonny Boy Williamson Vol. 2"
    BC 21 — "Big Joe Williams with Sonny Boy"
    BC 23 — "Jook Joint Blues, The 50's"
    BC 24 — "Sonny Boy Williamson Vol. 3"

BLUES OBSCURITIES BOE 2 — "Lonesome Harmonica"
    (Reissue of rare harp blues from 50's and 60's — Eddie
    Burns, Mojo Bofford, Ace Holder, Harmonica Fats, etc.
    — English import)

BLUESVILLE 1025 — Sonny Terry "Sonny's Story"

BYG 529 510 — Junior Wells, Buddy Guy, Otis Spann

CHESS 416 — Little Walter "Confessin' The Blues"
    CH 60014 — Little Walter "Boss Blues Harmonica"
    CH 60031 — Muddy Waters "Unk In Funk"

CRESCENDO GNP 10002 — Memphis Slim "The Blues Is
    Everywhere"
    GNP 10003 — "Sonny Boy Williamson and Memphis Slim
    In Paris"
    GNP 10006 — "Best of Jimmy Reed"

CONTEMPORARY 10031 — Jesse Fuller
    10039 — Jesse Fuller "The Lone Cat"
    10051 — Jesse Fuller "San Fransisco Bay Blues"

DELMARK 602 — Big Joe Williams "Piney Woods"
    608 — John Estes "Broke and Hungry"
    609 — Big Joe Williams, J.D. Short
    612 — Junior Wells "Hoodoo Man"
    622 — Carey Bell "Blues Harp"
    624 — "Chicago Ain't Nothin' But a Blues Band"
    628 — Junior Wells "South Side Blues Jam"
    635 — Junior Wells "On Tap"

DELTA LP 1000 — Big Walter Horton "King Of The Harmonica
    Players (Swedish import)

ELEKTRA EKL 240 — "The Blues, Rags and Hollers"
    7E-2001 — "Butterfield Blues Band Live"
    7E-2005 — "Golden Butter"
    EKS 7267 — "Lots More Blues, Rags and Hollers"
    EKS 7276 — "Old Time Banjo Project" (Only one harp cut)
    EKS 7294 — "Paul Butterfield Blues Band"
    EKS 74053 — "Butterfield Blues Band"

ENTERPRISE 1036 — Little Sonny "Hard Going Up"

FANTASY 24707 — Jesse Fuller "Brother Lowdown"
    24708 — Sonny Terry and Brownie McGhee "Back To New
    Orleans"

FOLK LEGACY FSA 18 — Arnold Keith Storm "Take The News
    To Mother"
    FSA 24 — Carolina Tar Heels

FOLKWAYS 2006 — "Sonny Terry's Washboard Band"
    2028 — Sonny Terry and Brownie McGhee "Get On Board
    Blues"
    2035 — "Sonny Terry"
    2201 — Seeger, McGhee and Terry "Washboard Band
    Country Dance Music"
    2327 — "Brownie McGhee and Sonny Terry"
    2369 — Sonny Terry "On The Road"
    2483 — "Woody Guthrie Sings Folk Songs, Vol. 1"
    2484 — "Woody Guthrie Sings Folk Songs, Vol. 2"
    2605 — "One-Man Band"
    2691 — Leadbelly, McGhee, Terry, Broonzy, F. Lewis and
    G. Cannon "Music Down Home"
    3817 — "Blues With Big Bill Broonzy, Sonny Terry,
    Brownie McGhee"
    3821 — "Sonny Terry's New Sound"

FORTUNE 3012 — "Blues Sound Of Hastings Street Era" (With
    Dr. Ross on harp)

GOOD TIME JAZZ 10031 — Jesse Fuller "Jazz Folk Songs,
    Spirituals, and Blues"

MILL CITY 172 — "Good Old Koerner, Ray And Glover"

MONUMENT KZ 32749 — Charlie McCoy "Fastest Harp In The
    South"
    KZ 32215 — Charlie McCoy "Good Time Charlie's Got The
    Blues"
    KZ 31910 — Charlie McCoy
    KZ 32922 — Charlie McCoy "Nashville Hit Man"
    Z 31329 — Charlie McCoy "Real McCoy"

MUSE 5008 — Muddy Waters "Mud In Your Ear"

MUSKADINE 101 — Joe Hill Louis "The One Man Band"

OLYMPIC 7108 — Brownie and Sonny "Hootin' and Hollerin'"
    7115 — Big Joe Williams with Lightnin' Hopkins, Brownie
    and Sonny "Blues Bash"

ORIGIN JAZZ LIBRARY 4 — "The Great Jug Bands"
    19 — "That Jug Band Sound"

POLYDOR PD 5014 — Shakey Jake Harris "The Devil's
    Harmonica"

POLYDOR/CARNIVAL (Juke Box Series — Import)
    2941-006 — George "Wild Child" Butler (Reissued from
    Jewel)

PRESTIGE PR 7368 — "Jesse Fuller's Favorites"
    PR 7715 — "Best Of Sonny Terry and Brownie McGhee"
    PR 7718 — Jesse Fuller "San Fransisco Bay Blues"

PURITAN 3003 — "The Great Original Recordings Of
    Harmonica Frank"

RBF RF 6 — "The Jug Bands"
    RF 8 — Sleepy John Estes (Several good cuts with Hammie
    Nixon)

RIMROCK 101 — "All The Family Favorites"

SONET 648 — J.D. Short (European import)

SPIVEY 1008 — The Muddy Waters Blues Band

STINSON SLPX 7 — "Chain Gang" (With Sonny Terry)

TESTAMENT T-2205 — Big Joe Williams with Willie Lee Harris
    "Back To The Country"
    T-2206 — Dr. Isaiah Ross "Call The Doctor"
    T-2220 — Chicago String Band
    T-2222 — "It Must Have Been The Devil" (Jack Owens
    with several cuts by Bud Spires)

TRADITION 1005 — "Instrumental Music Of The Southern
    Appalachians"

TRADITIONAL TLS 617 — Jean and Lee Schilling "Porches Of
    The Poor" (Some nice white style harmonica by Lee
    Schilling)

TRANSATLANTIC 1135 — Walter "Shakey" Horton with Hot
    Cottage

VANGUARD VSD 79153 — "Big City Blues"
    VSD 79163 — "Jug Band Music"
    VSD 79178 — John Hammond "So Many Roads"
    VSD 79198 — John Hammond "Country Blues"
    VSD 79216 — "Chicago — The Blues Today"
    VSD 79217 — "Chicago — The Blues Today"
    VSD 79218 — "Chicago — The Blues Today"
    VSD 79231 — Jr. Wells "It's My Life Baby"
    VSD 79232 — Charlie Musselwhite "Stand Back"
    VSD 79234 — Jim Kweskin and The Jug Band
    VSD 79235 — Siegel-Schwall Band
    VSD 79249 — "Say Siegel-Schwall"
    VSD 79270 — Best of Kweskin, Jim and Jug Band"

VOGUE CLVLXR 550 — Louisiana Red (French import)

XTRA 1135 — Walter "Shakey" Horton with Hot Cottage
    (Import)

George and Marilyn Heaps-Nelson

ALPHABETICAL INDEX OF SONGS

Page

THE END!
Photo by A. Rothstein, Library of Congress Collection